Your Naturally
Healthy
Home

Your Naturally
Healthy
Home

Stylish,
Safe,
Simple

Alan Berman

RODALE

DEBT OF GRATITUDE

A small number of prescient individuals began, some 30 years ago, to talk about new ways of living and to design solutions to problems that the rest of the world at the time didn't even know existed. Out on the fringe and ahead of their time, these ideas are today central to our future. Beside the groundbreaking work of those people, this book pales into insignificance. The list is long but those I can readily identify are: Christopher Alexander, Wendell Berry, Rachel Carson, Paul Ekins, Paul Ehrlich, Paul Hawken, Ivan Illich, Amory Lovins, Bill McKibben, D. Meadows, Victor Papanak, David Pearson, Sim Van Der Ryn, Fritz Schumacher, John Seymour, John Todd, and Robert and Brenda Vale.

Also deserving mention are the visionaries who started, among many organizations, The Sierra Club, Friends of the Earth, Greenpeace and the Centre for Alternative Technology. To these and many other eco-thinkers, the world owes an incalculable debt. Their achievement will be properly celebrated when the rest of us start putting in place the actions they have so long advocated.

PLEASE NOTE

Photographs do not purport to show interiors that are entirely safe but to illustrate some of the issues discussed that give existing buildings a greater degree of safety.

This book is not intended to replace specialist medical advice. The author makes no claim to medical expertise. Arguments propounded are based on a broad consensus of views from the sources listed and refer to the generality of materials and processes. In some cases the particulars of individual products might differ from the views expressed.

WE INSPIRE AND ENABLE PEOPLE TO IMPROVE
THEIR LIVES AND THE WORLD AROUND THEM

Simultaneously published by Frances Lincoln Limited, 4 Torriano Mews, Torriano Avenue, London NW5 2RZ

Copyright © Frances Lincoln Limited 2001
Text copyright © Alan Berman 2001
Acknowledgments appear on page 192

First Frances Lincoln edition: 2001

Alan Berman is hereby identified as the author of this work.

Printed and bound in Singapore

Library of Congress Cataloging-in-Publication Data

Berman, Alan.
    Your naturally healthy home : stylish, safe, simple / Alan Berman.—1st Frances Lincoln ed.
        p.   cm.
    Includes bibliographical references and index.
    ISBN 0–87596–931–3
    1. House construction.   2. Dwellings—Environmental engineering.   3. Housing and health.   4. Building materials—Environmental aspects.   5. Green products.   I. Title.
TH4812 .B473   2001
696—dc21   00–013199

Distributed in the book trade by St. Martin's Press

2   4   6   8   10   9   7   5   3   1

CONTENTS

INTRODUCTION

HOMEMAKING IS A CREATIVE ACT. It involves design decisions and choices that have always been guided by three principles: things in the home need to be practical, durable, and beautiful. The Romans called these principles "commodity," "firmness," and "delight." Today a fourth factor must be taken into account—safety. All design needs to be safe, both for our health and for that of the planet. This book aims to show that it is possible to create homes that are safe as well as attractive.

Before the advent in the 19th century of industries driven by fossil fuel, people made things in ways that by and large followed the biological patterns of nature, so they were safe for the environment. Resources used were naturally renewable, had few harmful side effects, and degraded safely when they became obsolete. Low demand meant that any damage to the earth was small, and in time any damage was generally repaired through natural processes. But today, the earth can no longer sustain the demands placed upon it. Progress and growth is driven by ever-increasing consumption, which generates increasing volumes of waste. Dirty factories powered by fossil fuels produce, on average, 10 pounds of waste for each pound of useful product they manufacture. We usually replace today's objects with tomorrow's, not because they have worn out, but because their appearance has become unfashionable—most consumer products become garbage after about 6 weeks.

NATURAL SOURCES

Locally made bricks and local wood made into boards and logs are natural, safe, and renewable sources *(above and above right)*.

Resources used were naturally renewable

In recent years, we've seen dramatic weather changes, along with increased risk of storm, flood, and fire. When our children can no longer safely sunbathe or swim in rivers, there can be little argument about the extent of human impact on the natural environment. The once finely tuned relationship between humankind and nature is clearly out of balance. We have arrived at the point of diminishing returns—the more we produce in our attempt to improve life, the more we destroy the capacity of the world to provide these improvements.

The destruction of global health is mirrored by a similar impact on our personal health. Tens of thousands of chemicals in use today in the home and elsewhere are known to

WOOD

The wooden walls of these New England houses are in harmony with the surrounding woods, from which materials have been culled.

LOCAL MATERIALS

These homes blend in with their settings. The sturdy walls of rural French houses *(below right)* have been built with stone found on the site. The rich reddish-brown of terra-cotta roofs in a Mediterranean village *(below left)* is the color of the local earth from which the tiles are made. Wood and cedar shingles from nearby forests were used for the sun-bleached decking and siding on a luxurious oceanfront veranda *(bottom)*.

be toxic. The alarming growth of 20th-century diseases—the increase in child asthma, for example—should at least cause us to wonder about the link between the chemicals that surround us and our health.

Ultimately, living in harmony with the earth requires that all homes are constructed with materials that are sustainable, that they consume as little energy as possible, and that they be safe. But most people cannot

SIMPLE, BASIC MATERIALS
Simple materials such as grasses and bamboo provide rich texture in homes *(above)*. New uses for basic materials challenge designers' ingenuity—this chair is made from recycled cardboard *(above right)*.

change the way in which their homes are constructed, and can only strive to make them as comfortable and safe as possible. The choice and quantities of materials used in home decorating makes a huge contribution to the safety and health of both planet and home. This book aims to outline a number of design strategies that can help make homes that are satisfying, while minimizing the impact on the environment and on our health.

REINTERPRETING DESIGN

First, we can develop an approach to design that is based on the way that people have built and decorated home for ages. Pre-industrial homes used local natural materials sparingly, functionally, and elegantly to make homes that were in tune with their local physical and climatic context. One rule of this local type of production recurs regularly in contemporary design—the idea of achieving more by using less. The most pleasing homes are often those in which economy and elegance of design create satisfying objects and maximize the enjoyment of space, light, and sunshine, together with the texture, color, and form of materials. In Chapter One, I explore different materials and elements used in the home and the lessons earlier, simpler cultures can teach us today.

Another strategy for safety is to use passive, low-energy techniques for making comfortable homes. Local materials and devices tuned to local climates have always done this—techniques that we have forgotten since comfort became available at the flick of a switch. Ways we can do this are discussed in Chapter Two.

NATURE'S CYCLES
Trees have simple needs: energy in the form of sunlight, and nutrient-rich soil for their roots to extract.

Further exciting opportunities for sustainability lie in the beginnings of a revolution that replaces materials made using dirty, wasteful methods with products made from clean processes. Manufacturing processes are being modeled on nature's cyclical patterns. Clean production can make objects that will biodegrade and become resources to use in the next cycle, thereby minimizing resource depletion and polluting wastes. Manufacturers in the United States and Germany in particular are demonstrating that such sustainable processes not only work but are economically viable. Safe materials and techniques, old and new, are explored in Chapter Three.

Many of the issues discussed in this book relate to risk. Just because we cannot see the dangerous effects of modern chemicals and electromagnetic radiation, for example, does not mean that they don't exist. Nor can we rely on producers to provide only products that

LESS IS MORE

This rich and interesting interior was created using a limited number of different elements. Natural materials are used for the floor, kitchen cabinets, and countertops.

are safe, when doing so may reduce their profits. Today we are exposed to a multiplicity of risks never before experienced. Our bodies may be likened to vessels that have evolved to hold a certain amount of toxic stress. But the risk is that at a certain point—and everyone's threshold will be different—they will hold no more and will overflow into illness.

Our buying and furnishing habits have worldwide impact on labor conditions and social and ethical issues, just as they do on environmental health. We need to take these issues into account, and while we cannot always know what happens in faraway countries, there are organizations that do. The "fair trade" labeling of products helps us to encourage and support ethical production practices.

Many of the demands for a safe home conflict with each other and with ethical issues. Responsible design needs to take into account the issues involved in design choice—personal circumstances, global and personal environmental health, transport issues, as well as ethical production. This book offers no simple answers and prescribes no particular design or style. Rather, it explores the more significant of these aspects, helping you to establish your own priorities for choice. Homes that are lastingly satisfying start a virtuous circle: There will be little reason to change them simply to follow fashion. Resource depletion and wasteful consumption will thereby be reduced. If this book helps to create just a few safe and comfortable homes that have less of an impact on the health of the earth, then it will have been worthwhile.

Chapter One
DESIGN AND ENVIRONMENT

NO HOME IS AN ISLAND

THE CHOICE OF ANY ITEM FOR YOUR HOME, such as a chair, floor covering, or paint, may seem like a straightforward decision. But dig a little deeper into the origins of that item and you'll uncover a vast web of global and personal health issues. At every stage—from the raw materials used, to manufacture and transport, and throughout its useful life until it is discarded—every household item has an impact on our environment and thus on our lives.

The global environmental crisis described in the introduction to this book stems from the fact that while nature works with benign and productive life cycles, industrial processes are usually destructive. Nature's cycles are like a closed loop—biological processes, fueled by the sun, create materials that grow and have a useful life until they biodegrade, becoming a resource from which new materials can grow. In contrast, many first-generation industrial processes are linear: They take resources, use energy to process them, and create short-lived products and by-products that end up as useless, often toxic, waste.

Every household **item** has an **impact** on our environment and our lives

Two simple chairs, both with classic designs, illustrate these differences: A traditional ladderback chair has solid wood legs, seat, and back; a second chair has a molded plywood seat and back, and chrome-plated steel legs.

The ladderback chair, whether a simple rough-hewn example or an elegant 18th-century Shaker version, was made from wood grown in local forests, which regenerate themselves naturally. The wood was taken to nearby workshops (sometimes within the forest itself), and the chair was made using simple tools that consumed a minimal amount of energy. The beeswax finish and any glues needed were animal-based products from local sources. Employing craftsmen living nearby sustained the local economy as well as the woodland. Any wood waste was used to make smaller items, as fuel, or in animal bedding. If the chair broke, it could—and still can—be repaired using simple skills. When it's finally disposed of, the whole chair will rot, producing safe and regenerative organic matter—an example of a closed-loop life cycle that does little damage to the environment.

Conversely, the plywood-and-steel chair has a negative impact on the environment. The steel for the legs uses iron ore—a finite resource that requires energy to mine, transport, and refine. More energy is used to take it to a factory where it is made into steel tubing. This is shipped to a fabrication shop, which sends it on again to be formed into legs that are sent away for chroming—a high-energy process that produces toxic waste. Meanwhile, in another part of the world, trees are cut down for the plywood seat. The wood is transported to huge machines for slicing into thin veneers that are then laminated together under heat and pressure, using dangerous chemical-based glues to bond the sheets into plywood. The plywood is taken to another factory where it is molded into the seat and back—again under considerable heat. Then the plywood parts are coated with a range of polyurethanes, PVCs (polyvinyl chlorides), and solvent coatings. When the plywood and steel parts finally meet, the result is a chair that is almost impossible to repair—although some steel may be recycled. When its relatively short useful life is over, the chair ends up in a landfill and leaches pollutants into the ground as the chemical glues and chrome degrade.

THE RIGHT CHOICES

Most of the items used to furnish and decorate our homes undergo a huge range of processes in their manufacture, including painting, staining, dyeing, printing, treating, and washing, as well as that huge waste generator—packaging.

Obviously, our design choices have a direct link to the global environment by consuming natural resources; using energy during both production and transport; creating by-product emissions that pollute the air, water, or ground; and in the longevity of any product in both its useful and waste states. While this doesn't mean our only choice is to live with a house full of antiques, we need to make smart choices for our homes.

Realizing that nearly every object used in making and furnishing a home has an impact on the environment makes the need for ecologically sound choices all too clear. There are essentially two positive approaches we can adopt in order to make safe, healthy homes and help the planet. We can take inspiration from traditional building techniques that have proved safe for centuries and existed before the industrial revolution, and we can seek out the growing number of exciting new products that are beginning to be developed by a new, 21st-century industrial revolution. Cleaner processes imitate nature's closed loop cycles to avoid resource depletion, waste, and pollution. Such methods make cleaner, safer products, paving the way to healthier homes —and a healthier planet.

ANCIENT AND MODERN
The old ladderback chair *(above)* is made of simple local materials and displays all the characteristics of traditional benign design. The bent plywood chair with chromed steel legs *(left)* is attractive, but many of its design features are typical of non-sustainable production.

FALLINGWATER
When designing "Fallingwater," *(previous pages)*, architect Frank Lloyd Wright used natural materials to create a home that is in harmony with its surroundings.

ENERGY AND POLLUTION

OUR LIFESTYLES TODAY RELY ON inexpensive energy derived from easily tapped fossil fuels. We use products derived from oil not only for light, warmth, and power, but also to run the vehicles that move us around and for the production of all the things we use. Measured in real terms, all this fuel costs the earth very dearly. Burning fossil fuel depletes the earth's natural resources, releases toxic emissions into the atmosphere, and pollutes our land and water. It also distorts the earth's naturally balanced climate patterns by damaging rain forests and oceans. Furthermore, cheap energy facilitates cheap production, which leads to higher levels of consumption. The consequences of this cycle include using more natural resources, generating more polluting emissions, and creating ever-greater volumes of waste. As well as decorating safely, it is essential to decorate with less.

The earth's stock of mineral resources is finite. Oil, gas, and coal have taken millions of years to form. Estimates vary, but at current rates it is likely that all the world's oil will last only to about the year 2050, natural gas until 2030, and coal until 2200. While there may be hidden reserves, extracting remote stocks becomes self-defeating because the more inaccessible they are, the more energy is needed to extract them. It is unrealistic to maintain that none of the world's resources should be used at all, but those that are used must come from properly managed sources and include the maximum amount of recycling. And the energy we use should come from the earth's natural, renewable, clean sources—the sun, wind, and oceans.

PETROCHEMICAL PRODUCTS

A by-product of the growth in energy consumption has been the expanding petrochemical industry, which now produces about 95 percent of all the chemicals in use today. These contain petrochemical derivatives, many of which are dangerous to our health. Most petrochemical-based products, of which plastics are the best-known examples, appear safe. Yet their production process and the waste created during production are indeed harmful. Because they are totally inert, most petrochemicals need to be combined with chlorine, an extremely dangerous chemical, to make them react in most manufacturing processes. Chlorine produces a wide variety of toxic emissions and polluting wastes that can't be recycled. When disposed of, these wastes emit further atmospheric, liquid, and solid pollutants.

AIR POLLUTION

Air pollution causes extensive environmental degradation by a host of chemical emissions. By far the most damaging are carbon monoxide, carbon dioxide, sulfuric acid, and nitrous oxide, which, together with chlorine, contribute to the destruction of ozone as well as disturbing the world's self-regulating climate systems. In nature, these substances exist in small, carefully balanced quantities in the earth's ecological system. But that balance is disturbed by the huge quantities produced during industrial processes and by the 26 percent of greenhouse gases emitted from households.

▶ **Carbon dioxide** is increasing in the atmosphere. The build-up acts like a huge blanket over the earth, trapping its heat and thereby causing global warming and affecting weather patterns. Every one of us contributes to this—residents of large areas, for example, each generate about 10 tons of carbon dioxide a year.

▶ **Carbon monoxide** is emitted by the incomplete combustion of fossil fuels for home heating, lighting, manufacturing, and transportation. It is colorless and odorless—but deadly because it inhibits the healthy functioning of human and animal organs and blood cells. When inhaled in confined spaces it is a known killer. It has been estimated that the average human adds 3 tons of

A NATURAL LANDSCAPE

Air, light, soil, water, and plant growth are all part of nature's self-regulating, cyclical system, which is threatened by human impact on the earth.

A SELF-RENEWING SYSTEM

On the forest floor, plants constantly biodegrade and are regenerated. This self-renewing system serves as an inspiration for the clean, sustainable manufacturing systems of the 21st century.

carbon monoxide a year to the atmosphere from the energy used for transportation, heating, and lighting.

▶ **Sulfur dioxide** is given off from many industrial processes and becomes sulfuric acid when it comes in contact with atmospheric moisture. Like nitrous oxide, it produces acid rain, which damages soil, waterways, lakes, and forests, as well as creating photochemical fogs. Studies have found increases in the incidence of illnesses (such as childhood cancer and cardiac failure) in areas of high sulfur dioxide pollution.

▶ **Nitrous oxide** also reacts with the volatile organic compounds (VOCs) that are present in many home decorating products. This generates a damaging form of ozone at low levels and causes respiratory irritations. At upper atmospheric levels where the ozone naturally remains largely constant, the ozone layer protects all life from the sun's harmful radiation. But when volatile organic solvents (chemicals such as methyl chloroform, carbon tetrachloride, halons, and methyl bromides) come into contact with the sun, they produce chlorine, which

destroys the ozone layer much more rapidly than the earth naturally generates it. Provided international agreements to reduce ozone-destroying emissions are adhered to, this destruction might be repaired within about 50 years.

WATER POLLUTION

Waterways are polluted by emissions from a number of processes, including the washing and cooling of mechanical equipment, the washing of fabrics and paper during production, and pesticide runoff from farming. The fast-growing microchip industry in particular discharges huge quantities of water polluted with toxins. Chemicals leaching from waste in landfill sites also pollute our water.

SOLID WASTE AND LAND POLLUTION

Solid waste is no less a concern. In the United States, every pound of consumer goods produced is said to result in 10 pounds of waste material—much of it containing dangerous chemicals. Worldwide the ratio averages one pound of product to eight pounds of waste. Only a small proportion of these by-products of our contemporary manufacturing processes can be absorbed by the earth's natural biodegrading systems. The rest must be stored in landfill sites, where it pollutes the underlying ground and water and generates polluting gases as it decomposes. If it is inciner-

ated rather than dumped, waste emits more dangerous chemicals, such as dioxins, into the atmosphere, which can damage health. For example, mothers living near waste incinerators have been shown to have a higher-than-normal level of contaminants in their breast milk.

Clearly, what we do in our homes contributes significantly to the ill health of the planet at a number of levels. There are two main actions we can take. First, use—and thus encourage manufacturers to make—products and materials that avoid causing environmental damage. Second, modify our patterns of consumption so we demand less product and thereby reduce the amount of waste. Homes can still be comfortable and attractive while consuming—and containing—less. The global environment will improve if everyone follows the 3R rules—Reduce, Repair, Recycle.

Taking these actions will also significantly reduce the amount of harmful chemicals that currently exist in our homes. Studies have shown that of the chemicals commonly used in buildings, 41 cause climate change, 18 cause ozone depletion, 85 create photochemical ozone, 7 create acid rain, 120 cause toxic emissions to air, and 53 to water. The effects of these chemicals are not confined to global pollution: They also adversely affect the air quality inside our homes, and thus the health of ourselves and our families.

SAFE DESIGN
Built with local materials, this home *(top)* displays many features of safe design and uses local, renewable wood for fuel.

DESIGNING WITH LESS
A minimalist bathroom *(above)* is a perfect example of how designing with less can create a powerful, positive look.

HOME AND HEALTH

This home was constructed according to ecologically sound principles. It is safe both for the environment and its occupants.

THE LINKS BETWEEN FURNISHING and decorating materials and the quality of indoor environments are no less strong than than their links to the global environment. In the industrialized world we spend as much as 90 percent of our time indoors, so the importance of a healthy indoor environment cannot be overestimated. Yet the quality of indoor air can be ten times worse than that of outside air—even in urban areas. Thus we need to minimize indoor air pollution and ensure that our homes have plenty of fresh air and natural light.

The U.S. Environmental Protection Agency (EPA) considers indoor air quality one of the greatest single factors contributing to ill health, but this fact has barely been acknowledged—until recently. Studies of indoor environments suggest that many modern materials and chemicals contribute to a growing list of environmentally induced illnesses. It is also estimated that the dozens of potentially harmful chemicals in our homes can be up to 1,600 times more potent when combined.

Without a bad smell to alert us, we usually are unaware of poor indoor air quality. But just because we don't smell them does not mean that pollutants aren't present. Just as foods contain an increasing number of tasteless but harmful additives, modern building and decorating materials, too, have a complex mixture of chemical ingredients. Our homes are filled with potential dangers from a wide range of unsuspected sources, including:

▶ Cleaning materials, cosmetics, and garden pesticides
▶ Carpets glued with solvents, treated with fungicides, and containing residual pesticides
▶ Fabrics treated with chlorine, benzine, and/or formaldehyde
▶ Plywood and particleboard, which contain formaldehyde, urea, and other dangerous glues
▶ Paints and stains, which contain fungicides, volatile organic compounds (VOCs), and other chemicals
▶ Vinyl flooring, furniture, and plastics that contain VOCs such as bromines and chlorine

This home was constructed according to ecologically sound principles. It is safe both for the environment and its occupants.

XTRA SPACE

sunroom adds living space
d collects solar heat, which
lps keep cold air out.

NATURAL PAINT

The light-colored walls and
ceilings near the windows are
painted using organic,
vegetable-based paints.

EFFICIENT HEATING

The radiator positioned in the
middle of the living space
provides efficient heat
distribution.

SAFE CABINETS

Kitchen cabinets made of
granite on top of plywood
replace the usual laminate-
topped particleboard.

RECYCLED MATERIALS

This floor is made of reclaimed
oak boards. The structural
columns are untreated tree
trunks.

Yet humans have inhabited homes for centuries without encountering such problems. This may be because tradition-al homes were usually made with materials taken from their immediate surroundings—locally grown, pesticide-free wood, fabric colored with natural plant dyes, wood finishes containing beeswax, and floors made of local stone. But new materials have radically altered our home environment. Our bodies are ill-equipped to cope with the impact of all these new chemicals, many of which give off pollutants.

Fortunately, most people have immune systems that are strong enough to cope with toxic stress. But the longer you are exposed to these stresses, and the less sound your general immune system, the greater the likelihood of becoming ill. The alarming growth of many illnesses seems to bear this out: asthma, allergic reactions, respiratory ail-ments and diseases, and cancers were not present to the same extent in previous generations.

INDOOR AIR QUALITY

Two factors have coincided to create much of today's dan-gerous indoor air quality. The first is the development of new materials used in home construction since the end of World War II. Cheap, quickly built mass housing exploited the new, often lightweight materials and processes offered by the petrochemical industry. What wasn't understood at the time was that any of these materials release chemicals into the air—a process called offgassing.

The second factor has been the desire since the 1970s to conserve energy, with two consequences. First, energy consumption was reduced by increasing insulation in buildings, using mainly petrochemical products such as foamed polymeric insulation materials. This was coupled with a drive to seal houses tightly and prevent the loss of all the warm air that we heat with such high energy costs. Fireplaces and all the drafty nooks and crannies were

blocked up, eliminating ventilation. This seals in not only human-generated germs, toxins, and moisture, but also the vast number of chemicals that are vaporized and off-gassed into the home's now unchanging air. Indoor air, stagnant for longer periods, spirals down in quality. So-called advanced building technology has created home environments with previously unknown dangers, and it has taken 20 or more years for these problems to be fully appreciated.

CAUSES OF POOR INDOOR AIR QUALITY

Poor indoor air has four main causes: offgassing of chemicals, particulates, combustion gases, and electromagnetic radiation. Each of these causes can can trigger a variety of physiological reactions such as eye, nose, and throat irritations; congestion; fatigue; headaches; respiratory disorders; and allergic reactions. For a list of the more common

materials and their chemical makeup, and a discussion of their suspected health effects, see page 180.

Offgassing (or outgassing) from materials is the slow release into the atmosphere—similar to evaporation—of chemicals that vaporize either from the material itself or from chemical residues used in manufacturing processes. The chemicals may be naturally unstable or may be released through aging or by the effect of light, moisture, or abrasion. Chemicals commonly emitted into the atmosphere in this way include the dangerous group known as VOCs (volatile organic compounds) and many other petrochemical derivatives such as benzine, naphtha, formaldehyde, organochlorines, phenols, and the organophosphates contained in PVCs. Toxic metals, such as lead, mercury, cadmium, and zinc, also offgass—and they can cause particularly severe contamination when they are in contact with water or other particulates. Materials commonly used in our homes that contain these chemicals include plywood, particleboard, insulation, carpeting, vinyl flooring adhesives, paints, and fabrics (see Chapter Three).

Particulate and biological contaminants are an important element of poor air quality. All atmospheres contain very fine, invisible airborne particles, most often including general household dust, animal hair and dander, microorganisms, pollens and mold spores, as well as smoke and asbestos. Molds in particular can be poisonous. Particulates can trigger a range of reactions in the immune system, including eczema, hay fever, and the restriction of breathing passages (which causes asthma and respiratory problems). The World Health Organization (WHO) maintains that the threshold below which particulates are safe is so low as to be barely measurable. One survey suggests that 6.5 percent of all cardiopulmonary deaths in the United States are due to particulate air pollution.

Combustion gases can be emitted by old, faulty, or badly maintained heating systems. Furnaces and water heaters that only partially burn their fuels emit gaseous residues such as nitrogen dioxide, carbon monoxide, and sulfur dioxide into the air. Carbon monoxide poisoning in the home can kill and it leads to a large number of symptoms often assumed to be the flu. Research has shown that carbon monoxide can impair cognitive functions and has also revealed links to lung disease. Test your furnace to make sure that it's burning properly.

Electromagnetic fields are perhaps the most contentious of domestic hazards. Electricity and electrical installations surround us everywhere in increasing numbers, and there is growing concern that these fields upset many of the body's finely balanced natural electrochemical functions. There are two kinds of radiation: low frequency electrical fields emitted from electrical cables and equipment, and the magnetic fields emitted from all appliances and equipment—which are considered the most dangerous. So extensive is the growing evidence against them that some countries have begun to legislate against potential dangers.

Despite all these problems, there are ways of making homes that are healthy to live in and do not damage the earth. Here are the main strategies, all of which are explained later in this book:

▶ Minimize energy consumption in your home to reduce consumption of fossil fuels.

▶ Decorate in a style that uses fewer rather than more items, and purchase these locally.

▶ Choose materials, both old and new, that do not damage the environment: The less processed a material, the safer it is likely to be.

▶ Select materials that do not offgas and damage indoor air quality.

▶ Ensure that all heating equipment, stoves, and fireplaces are properly serviced and maintained.

▶ Ventilate interiors to ensure constant fresh air, using a range of nonmechanical techniques.

▶ Make your home as well-lit and noise-free as possible.

▶ Use plants to counteract indoor pollution.

A SIMPLE INTERIOR

Rich textures combine with deliberately sparse
furnishings to create a calm, attractive space in
this home *(left)* that is made of local, renewable,
biodegradable materials.

OLD AND NEW

Different materials blend harmoniously in this
room *(below)*. Stone floors create a visual link to
the outside, compliment the bold wood structure,
and set off the delicate furniture.

TRADITIONAL DESIGN

PRE-INDUSTRIAL MATERIALS AND DESIGNS are generally more environmentally sound than materials developed by modern industrial processes. Now, at the beginning of the 21st century, we have discovered that there are lessons to be learned from the design principles of pre-industrial cultures. While still beautiful, these uncomplicated designs had little or no impact on the environment as a result of their simplicity. Traditional cultures conserved natural resources by using the simplest materials and forms—not so different from the modern slogans "form follows function" and "less is more." Design does not need to be complex to be beautiful.

FOLK AND TRADITIONAL STYLES

Regional approaches to homemaking have always unwittingly embodied principles that are essentially kind to the environment, and these are still valid today: Materials were obtained locally and used with care; they were natural, renewable, and safe when discarded. Basic but effective methods were used to heat and ventilate interiors. While today this is done using energy-greedy equipment, builders in the past exploited the qualities of local mate-

rials for their climate-modifying benefits. In desert areas, for example, thick walls made of local desert mud keep interior temperatures cool by absorbing the sun's heat. Then, in the cool nights the warm walls radiate some of the heat absorbed during the day into the house. In forested areas, roofs of solid logs covered with grass act as efficient insulators, while in wooded tropics timber-frame construction allows homes to be open to cooling breezes.

Traditional materials that have survived the test of time still satisfy us with their unsophisticated beauty. Simple, unadorned interiors are so much more than an assembly of fashionable shapes and colors. The lasting qualities of natural materials, such as flagstone, terra-cotta tiles, and wood-paneled walls, are derived in part from their connection with the local landscape and local skills, as well as the meanings and messages they carry about continuing traditions of homemaking.

By contrast, many of today's homes lack this sense of coherence and relationship to their surroundings. Instead, they are a product of a "pick and mix" approach to design, made possible by widely available materials as well as seductive images of styles from all over the world. The

ROUGH-HEWN STONE

Natural materials left unadorned link a home to its natural environment.

BAMBOO

Safe and renewable, bamboo is a distinctive building material.

WOOD

Wood is strong, safe, renewable, and a good insulator.

BRICK

Brick made of local clay lends an earthy appearance to an exterior.

These Norwegian homes *(left)* derive their beauty from environmentally sound building principles and the use of local materials. Log walls and earth-covered roofs provide excellent insulation and create dwellings that are part of the landscape. While a log house may not be for you, the interior of the Frank Lloyd Wright house "Fallingwater" *(below)* shows another example of how the bold use of local materials can tie a building to its surroundings.

NATURAL MATERIALS
Cork, shown here before processing, is a versatile, renewable floor or wall covering.

USING YOUR ENVIRONMENT
This outdoor dining area *(right)* with a deck made of local wood blends well with its wooded surroundings.

mass production and standardization of homes leaves little room for regional variation—those enjoyable differences between one house and another. This eclectic post-modern approach may be fashionable at times, but the almost universal admiration for traditional styles suggests that most of us have a need for the kind of permanence and connection to local context enjoyed by our ancestors. The use of traditional techniques and materials is one way of regaining this joy.

Clearly, the idea of using only local materials cannot be sustained in today's global economy, but the concept of "appropriate" materials is still valid. For example, in areas where wood is a common construction material, wooden flooring will make a more natural choice than other materials. Marble or mosaic tile, however beautiful, may seem out of place. But beyond selecting materials for their appropriateness to the context, we need to also think about the environmental impact our choices have. However appropriate the material, we must be sure that its production, transport, and other aspects are easy on the

environment. These ideas may narrow your range of choices, but they also suggest an expansion of traditional principles to fit today's global world.

One of the most difficult of these issues is that of employment conditions. If we apply the same criteria that we value in our society to production conditions in less-developed countries, we can expand the concept of well-meaning local employment into today's global context. An example might be a retailer of home furnishings in the developed world who insists that his third-world suppliers reduce child working hours and provide schooling and health care, which the retailer (and ultimately, the consumer) subsidizes. If the buying power of developed countries increases the trade of such manufacturers, then other manufacturers will be obliged to follow, creating a gentler circle of production.

ORIGINAL ARTS AND CRAFTS

This classic Edwin Lutyens Arts and Crafts interior *(left)* shows a sophisticated interpretation of English building. The structure and finishes use local brick and solid oak.

MODERN ARTS AND CRAFTS

A modern version of the Arts and Crafts style *(above)* still incorporates solid and durable materials and avoids superfluous decoration.

A NEW APPROACH

As much as we might wish to return to locally based designs, simply emulating them with modern materials is not enough. Traditional design has deep-rooted principles, but these must be augmented with new materials and technologies that are more beneficial to the environment. Aspects of production that suited people in the pre-industrial age must be updated for the 21st century.

NEW TECHNOLOGY

MAGINATIVE SCIENTISTS AND MANUFACTURERS ARE realizing that the destructive patterns of most 19th- and 20th-century industries are unsustainable. These industrial revolution processes are linear and dirty: They take the earth's natural resources and use considerable amounts of energy to make a product and its waste—waste that can be so dangerous that they make other parts of nature's potential resources unusable. But we are at the dawn of a new industrial revolution that is spawning new clean production methods that mimic the earth's organic processes. These are cyclical, using safe, renewable resources that are organically generated. Most waste goes toward regeneration of new products—just as waste food becomes compost for growing more plants. Environmental aspects of these new processes include:

▶ Replacing petrochemical products with naturally occurring ones that are non-hazardous, unprocessed, and preferably renewable, such as natural paints, lime plasters, and cork floors

▶ Using raw materials from the maximum number of species of plants or types of resources to reduce impact and allow regeneration

▶ Using raw materials located close to production

▶ Using renewable energy, such as solar and wind power, and of heat recovery techniques in processing equipment to allow the recycling of energy

▶ Extending product life by the recycling, disassembly, and reuse of components

▶ Recycling waste to become the ingredients of secondary and even tertiary products

This new "benign" approach to manufacturing processes is sometimes referred to as "biomimicry," and it holds enormous potential for a safer future. Environmentally benign materials being made in this way include carpets from

DIRTY INDUSTRY/LINEAR MANUFACTURING

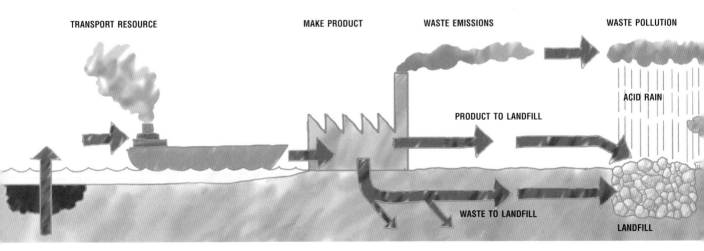

TRANSPORT RESOURCE   MAKE PRODUCT   WASTE EMISSIONS   WASTE POLLUTION

ACID RAIN

PRODUCT TO LANDFILL

WASTE TO LANDFILL   LANDFILL

OIL RESOURCE

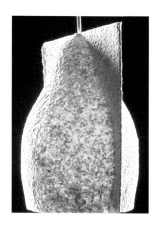

RECYCLED SHADE

This unique lamp shade *(left)* was made from paper pulp produced from recycled paper.

"CLEAN" TEXTILES

interesting fabrics *(right)* can be made using techniques that don't produce polluting emissions and chemical residues.

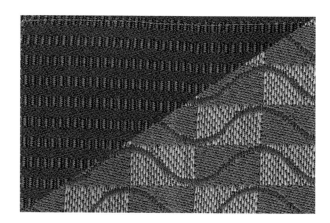

recycled plastic bottles, paints from vegetable extracts, tiles from crushed ceramic waste, rubber flooring from recycled tires, plastic from plant-based cellulose, and self-colored cottons that need no additional dyes.

Typical of the new clean processes are Climatex Lifecycle fabrics, which have set a new standard of environmental safety. Made by the pioneering company DesignTex, Climatex Lifecycle is made from worsted wool and ramie—both biodegradable yarns. Fabric trimmings and scraps are used by farmers instead of plastic for weed-suppressing covers on the soil. This fabric gradually decays and provides organic nutrients just like any other biodegradable waste. The DesignTex factory in Switzerland claims to use only drinking-quality water in its processes, and returns the water in the same quality at the end of the production cycle. The company surveyed 8,000 chemicals for potential use and found only 38 to be sufficiently free from known or suspected toxic or otherwise dangerous effects. The company has become a model for manufacturers worldwide.

SUSTAINABLE INDUSTRY/CLOSED-LOOP CYCLE

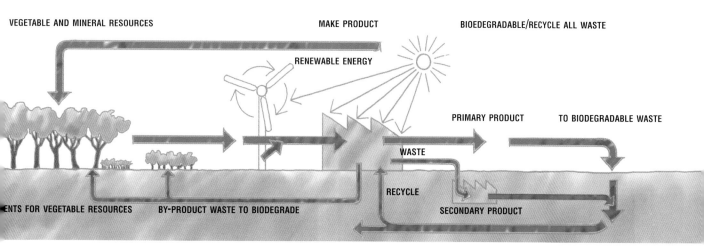

VEGETABLE AND MINERAL RESOURCES

MAKE PRODUCT

BIOEDEGRADABLE/RECYCLE ALL WASTE

RENEWABLE ENERGY

PRIMARY PRODUCT

TO BIODEGRADABLE WASTE

WASTE

RECYCLE

SECONDARY PRODUCT

ENTS FOR VEGETABLE RESOURCES

BY-PRODUCT WASTE TO BIODEGRADE

While the range of such products is small at present, it is growing as manufacturers begin to realize that in the long term, clean processing will prove more, rather than less, profitable. Together with the acceptance of the still untapped potential of renewable energy, these are enormously positive signs for the future.

Creative re-evaluation of modern production is also leading to a new look at patterns of trade. Some companies are beginning to think in wider environmental terms, such as planting trees to absorb the same amount of carbon dioxide they pump into the air through when transporting their goods. An international carpet company now leases instead of sells its product to the customer. Credit is given for the worn carpet, which is taken away and recycled to make a lower-grade product to be sold to another customer, and so on. There is a shift to services rather than products, creating the attitude—"don't own it, use it."

THE VALUE OF THE WORLD WIDE WEB

Twenty-first century technology makes clean production possible, and it also makes it easier to find out about the products we use. The Internet now gives everyone access to information, making it possible to check the chemical ingredients of a product or the environmental credentials of almost any company. Details of the methods used by a California furniture workshop or a Swiss textile mill will never make the shelves of your local library, but they are increasingly available at the click of a mouse. As more and more businesses post details of their products on the Web, finding the nearest, safest, or least-polluting source of an item becomes ever easier.

Exposing the polluting practices of manufacturers is another important element of this growing environmental information. Many government agencies—both central and local—keep track of the activities of companies and publicize breaches of environmental controls. This has two effects: First, it is harder for companies to hide poor environmental policies; and second, the process of "naming and shaming" will force companies to clean up their environmental performance. They may do so for economic reasons, but what counts in the end is that they damage the environment less.

The Web also offers scrutiny of ethical performance. In the new global supermarket, the buying power of each and every individual is one of the few significant constraints on unscrupulous corporations: If no one buys tropical hard-

SUSTAINABLE FOREST
Bamboo *(far left)* is a sustainable material that grows six times faster than most hardwoods.

CALIFORNIA WIND FARM
Generating electricity from renewable resources *(left)* avoids the depletion of fossil fuels.

ETHICAL CONSIDERATIONS
Importers of goods from developing countries need to look closely at working practices *(below)* to determine whether the labor conditions during production are safe and humane.

woods the rainforest will survive; if no one uses PVC products or paints that are high in VOCs, significant toxic emissions will be reduced. This has been proven by a campaign mounted by student organizations, labor unions, and other concerned groups in the United States to improve the extremely poor working conditions in the international garment industry. They formed the Fair Labor Association, which insists on certain employment standards in factories around the world. If any manufacturer does not treat his employees fairly, his survival is threatened through negative publicity on the Internet. Garments made by factories that comply with the regulations now carry the association's label.

Today we can combine the timeless and beautiful functionalism of traditional design and techniques with the products of new, clean technology and develop a safe ecological style suitable for our post-industrial age. Instead of selecting materials that simply reflect current fashions, selection can be based on the realities behind every material or product—from its source through its whole life cycle. This benign design approach will create individual homes in tune with their cultural and physical context, which will keep you safe and not degrade the planet.

EVALUATING MATERIALS

How can we select materials that are safe for both personal and environmental health? The issues touched on so far demonstrate that every material or product needs to satisfy criteria about its source, manufacture, health consequences, and behavior as waste. With eco-labeling systems (see page 178) attached to very few decorating materials, we need to ask suppliers and manufacturers about their products.

Environmental issues are so multifaceted that despite the considerable research taking place no absolute standard has been established. The organizations that have developed eco-labeling systems apply different criteria. But while experts argue about differences of detail, all agree on the main issues that need to be evaluated:

▶ The depletion of natural resources caused by the making of a product

▶ The amount of energy consumed in the production or processing of a product—known as its embodied energy

▶ The extent of pollutants emitted during manufacture

▶ A product's impact on indoor air quality and health

▶ A product's ability to biodegrade harmlessly, or its potential for recycling

▶ Ethical issues affecting the community that makes a product

These criteria form the basis of the charts detailing the environmental credentials of some of the materials discussed in Chapter Three.

DEPLETION OF NATURAL RESOURCES

The issue here is the extent to which extracting a material exhausts the supply for future generations. The stock of natural resources (other than those regenerated through vegetative growth) is finite, and strategies are needed to reorient production to renewable resources—essentially those fueled by the sun's energy. But extracting even some of these renewable resources may cause damaging environmental consequences that warrant protection of the resource. For example, hardwood trees from tropical rain

CORK HARVEST

In some Mediterranean areas, cork is a staple industry. Buying habits in the rest of the world can affect the stability of local communities.

forests can be regrown—although slowly—when cut down. But their loss deprives unique flora and fauna of their habitats, as well as possibly causing earth erosion. The forests where these trees grow also provide the earth's greatest "sponge" for absorbing greenhouse gasses.

EMBODIED ENERGY

This is the amount of energy consumed by extracting the raw materials for a product, including all aspects of its processing, manufacture, and transport. Transportation from point of sale to point of use is also part of the equation.

POLLUTING EMISSIONS

Emissions are the amount of polluting waste released into the atmosphere, land, or water from all aspects of the processing or manufacture of a product. This includes pollution from burning fossil fuels. It is important to remember the simple rule that the closer a material remains to its natural state, the less processing needs to take place, and the less the impact on the environment.

INDOOR AIR QUALITY

This evaluates the impact materials have on indoor air and, therefore, health. While there are many different ways materials can affect indoor air quality, for practical purposes they are all grouped together. Even if a material has little impact across a range of consequences, just one potentially harmful effect makes it unsatisfactory.

RECYCLING POTENTIAL AND WASTE GENERATION

These issues include the ability of a material or product to biodegrade safely or be recycled when it has completed its useful life. Recycling takes three forms: First, an item can be reused in its original state; second, it may be reprocessed to form new materials (for example, plastic bottles that are reprocessed to become carpet fibers); third, it may be disassembled and its components reused.

ETHICAL ISSUES

The demand for inexpensive goods in the developed world has enormous social consequences and can lead to hopelessly inadequate working conditions—even slavery. It is vital to evaluate manufacturers' attention to matters such

SLATE QUARRYING
Slate *(above)* is a safe, durable material that can be reused often.

CLAY TILES
These roof tiles *(above right)* are made from local clay.

as child labor, fair wages, educational programs, and health, safety, and gender issues. Ask questions and look for the labels that certify acceptable standards (see page 33).

OTHER FACTORS

Each material and the various ways in which it is used will raise unique issues that cannot be generalized. For an assessment of environmental and health issues to be meaningful in your own circumstances, you may need to ask additional specific questions. What methods and materials are used for packing? What dangers are posed by work on the material outside factory conditions? Do the cleaning requirements pose environmental problems? What is the impact on individuals with particular health sensitivities?

Everyone is likely to place different weight on different criteria, so developing a set of personal priorities will lead to very personal selections. This will create a home that is not only safer for the environment and your health but also expresses your own personality and values.

RECYCLED PLASTICS

This practical tabletop *(below)* is
made from recycled plastic bottles.

Chapter Two

LIGHT, HEAT, AND AIR

LIGHT

A LIGHT-FILLED ROOM

Large windows flood the room with light, thanks to their height and depth.

THE PLAY OF LIGHT ON SURFACES, shapes, and textures creates the "poetry" of space. Light casts shadows, gives definition to form, and creates mood and atmosphere. The manipulation of light is one of the most powerful tools for making a successful interior.

Without light, life would not exist. Like plants, humans depend on light as a source of energy—directly and indirectly, all living things are driven by light from the sun. For humans, this dependence is not only physiological but also emotional—sunlight cheers, grayness depresses. For a home to be healthy and feel happy and comfortable, it needs as much natural light as possible.

The importance of natural light tends to be forgotten today, when electricity allows us to work 24 hours a day, even at times when our biological clocks are urging us to sleep. As a species, humans evolved to function according to the rhythms of outdoor light, yet many of us now spend as much as 90 percent of our time indoors, effectively in permanent gloom.

Light is measured in units called lux. One lux is equivalent to the light of one candle. A bright, sunny day measures up to 80,000 lux; even an overcast gray sky can equal 10,000 lux. In contrast, the recommended level of light for working indoors is between 300 and 500 lux, and general light levels in our homes are usually about 250 lux.

Our need for natural light is illustrated by accumulating evidence of the effects of low levels of light on health. One example is the condition known as SAD—Seasonal Affective Disorder—which especially affects people living in northern latitudes, where winter days are short and light levels are low for months at a time. SAD causes severe depression and lethargy in sufferers, but can be relieved by regular doses of bright light from a specially designed light box. These boxes contain full-spectrum lights—lights that are as close as possible to natural daylight.

The message for the homeowner is simple: Your home, both literally and metaphorically, should be as light and sunny as possible. Aim to always increase the amount of light in your home and to use decorative effects to enhance apparent brightness. In many homes, improvements in light levels can be made with a small amount of self-contained building work that causes little disruption.

BRING LIGHT INTO YOUR HOME

There is a distinction between sunlight and daylight. Sunlight is direct sun, while daylight is cast by the sky—and is received either directly or indirectly. Each has different color qualities and intensity.

Sky brightness and sunlight angles vary according to location. The higher the sun is in the sky, the brighter and hotter its rays are. In northern European countries, sunlight angles are much lower than those in southern Europe and most of North America. Although weaker and less hot, low-angled sunlight penetrates deeper into a room—a benefit in northern latitudes. In areas with higher sun angles and strong heat, screening and filtering light becomes more important to protect the home from too much brightness at midday and in high summer.

Traditional buildings all over the world use an array of devices for controlling the amount of light entering a building. Regardless of the numerous variations in design, however, there are five main options for making the best use of light:
▶ Allocate rooms to maximize natural light at different times of day.
▶ Add transparency—create views from one room to another.
▶ Increase the amount of light coming in.
▶ Use reflected light.
▶ Add screens of various kinds to modify or filter light.

The role of glass is fundamental in creating light in the home and for controlling heat loss and heat gain. It also offers a wealth of decorative opportunities. For more details on the practical aspects of using glass, see page 140.

POSITIONING ROOMS

▶ Look at how the sun travels around your home and, if possible, match the use of rooms to the sun's path. For example, bedrooms should face east to catch the morning sun, and living rooms south or west to receive afternoon and mid-morning sun. Use darker rooms less frequently or only at night.

▶ Don't assume that a room designated a living room or bedroom must always be used as such. You will get great pleasure every day waking up in a sun-filled east-facing room, even if it is smaller than a north-facing room that the previous homeowners used as their master bedroom.

ADDING TRANSPARENCY

▶ Windows in internal walls or glazed screens between areas can illuminate one space by "borrowing" light from another. If privacy is needed, use screens of opaque glass, which cast diffused light, or hang blinds to cover clear glass. Japanese designers have mastered the art of creating soft, diffused light by using rice paper *shoji* screens, which have a calming, peaceful effect.

▶ Extra areas of transparency within a dwelling bring a feeling of light and space. If you're planning new construction, consider stopping solid walls short of meeting at corners, and fill the gap with a strip of glass.

SCREENED LIGHT

Translucent screens allow a soft, gentle light to filter in from the next room. Although separate, the spaces are visually connected by the light.

This will allow light from one room into another and create the sculptural impression of walls floating in space. Gain maximum effect by setting the glass into the wall surface without any frame, and treat different wall planes with different colors or textures. Art nouveau interiors are particularly rich in transparency, using internal screens and colored glass to give spaces a warm, glowing richness.

▶ Glimpses of sunlight on walls or floors seen from north-facing rooms will significantly improve the sense of brightness. Do this simply by changing a solid door into one with a window, and use blinds or opaque, sandblasted, or acid-etched glass for privacy.

INCREASING LIGHT

▶ With relatively minor construction work, windows can be altered, bringing radical improvements to a home. For example, it is reasonably easy to lower a windowsill and create a full-length window that allows light to flood the floor and reflect up into the room.

▶ The higher a window, the more light it will throw into the room. Increase the height of existing windows or, in a high-ceilinged room, add small, high windows in one wall. These windows do not need to be opened, so they can be made simply of glass set in frames. They don't even need curtains.

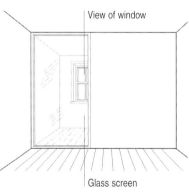

View of window

Glass screen

TRANSPARENCY

Replacing part of a wall with glass *(above and left)* creates internal views and a feeling of openness and light. When the glass wall is part of a corner, a previously dark room can benefit from an adjacent, lighter space.

Window frames painted black act like picture frames to draw the eye into the garden *(left)*. The connection between inside and out is further emphasized by the continuous, light-reflecting flooring.

The mirrors below the skylight *(above)* help maximize the light in this attic room. The wood framing and paneling reflects warm, soft light.

Oriole   Bay

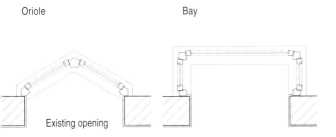

Existing opening

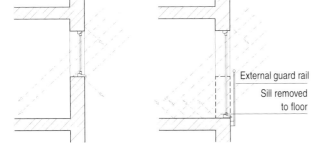

External guard rail
Sill removed to floor

External guard rail

Sill removed
to floor

WINDOW SHAPES

Without altering the structure of a window opening, it is possible to add an oriole window or a square bay to create a light-filled extension to a room. Add an attractive seat to a bay window.

▶ You can change the shape of a window without altering the structural opening in the wall. Replace a flat window with either a square projecting bay, or an oriole (see above). This can make a light-filled area and, if the sill is low enough, a window seat.

▶ Use skylights to brighten dark areas at the top of a house. Because the light from the sky directly overhead is so much brighter than the light from the horizon, even a small skylight is highly effective. If you have the good fortune to be on the top floor of an apartment building, obtain permission to install skylights. Make sure that they are double- or triple-paned to prevent condensation from rising warm air.

▶ On upper floors or in apartments (if you can get permission), an excellent way to create a feeling of airiness is to make inward-opening French windows down to the floor and protect the opening with a set of railings for safety. These "Romeo and Juliet" balconies are common in many traditional European buildings and transform even the dullest room into one that is filled with light.

▶ "Light tubes" are simple to install—these small, tubular skylights work on the same principle as a periscope. As small as 12 inches in diameter, they can bend to funnel bright daylight from the roof opening down into a room

FRENCH WINDOWS

The easiest part of a window to alter is the wall beneath the sill. Removing the sill beneath a window and installing French doors will make the whole room feel like a balcony and allows light to enter the room and bounce off the floor. A protective railing is placed outside the wall line for safety. These structures are sometimes called Romeo and Juliet balconies (left).

or other space. Light tubes can be taken through two floors—although finding a route is not always easy.

▶ Tiny glass inserts no larger than one or two bricks set in outside walls bring in shafts of light and can greatly enliven a gloomy interior. Sixteenth-century Turkish bathhouses had roofs inset with glass lenses, creating wonderful diffused light. Or take a cue from John Soane, an English architect who was a master of the art of bringing daylight to interiors. He used hidden skylights to throw light onto richly colored wall surfaces, often reflecting it in mirrors to create spaces of infinite luminosity, even in the darkest interiors.

▶ One of the best ways to create a light-filled room is to add a sunroom. Properly designed, they can create bright, semi-outdoor spaces and can also function as a valuable source of solar heat (see page 66).

A CALMING LIGHT

This large space *(left)* is suffused with even light that is characteristic of north-facing skylights. Light enters from two opposite sides of the room, creating a balanced, calm atmosphere.

A VARIETY OF EFFECTS

Different sizes and styles of window give very different light effects in this room *(right).* A large opening on the left gives overall lighting, while a small glass pane in the wall provides a sharply focused beam. Delicate points of light come from the lattice on the far wall.

REFLECTED LIGHT

▶ Maximize the effect of whatever natural light does enter your room by keeping floor surfaces near the window a light color so that they bounce daylight deep into the room. However, where you have a stone or tile floor you may want to use dark colors on surfaces near windows so that the floor absorbs heat (see page 66).

▶ Light-colored furnishings and other flat surfaces (such as a tabletop near the window) give a greater impression of light than darker-colored ones.

▶ Mullions, which divide a window into smaller panes, can add to the luminescence in a space. Light bounces off them and increases the apparent brightness. Traditional mullions painted white and Venetian blinds both create this feeling of lightness—provided they are thin enough. Many modern windows lose this quality because of overly dominant mullions.

▶ The window surround (or cheeks) is important for reflecting light into the room—old windows set deep into thick walls are particularly effective. The shutters

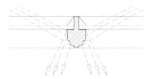

Light reflecting off mullion

MULLIONS

Large, clear sheets of glass are not necessarily the most attractive windows. Traditional mullions *(above and right)* reflect light to create a luminous foreground screen that can brighten a room.

PROTECTIVE BLINDS
Delicate blinds over this expanse of glass *(above)* provide an element of privacy without affecting the view. They also offer protection from strong sunlight and glare.

A LIGHT CORNER
In this room *(right)*, light reflects off the sides of the deep walls, the skylights, and the wide window seat—an inviting place to sit. Thin window frames emphasize the solid masonry.

This small opening in a modern room *(below)* emulates a traditional, deep window. The sides reflect the light, making the opening seem larger while focusing the view.

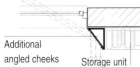

Additional
angled cheeks   Storage unit

REFLECTING MAXIMUM LIGHT

Increase the cheeks on either side of an opening *(above)* so that the windows appear to be set in thick walls that reflect light into the room. This can be done by increasing the depth of the fittings or insulation.

surrounding windows of some 19th-century houses also reflect light, yet many people lose this effect by stripping the shutters back to the natural wood.

▶ Where deep walls are not available, the same effect can be created by making deep "cheeks" around the windows. To do this, bring the sides of cupboards or bookcases—preferably with an angled surface—tight up to the sides of the window. The depth of the unit will extend the depth of the window jamb.

▶ On tall windows, add high-level window shelves that catch the light and reflect it onto the ceiling. This is particularly effective in deep rooms.

The light entering these rooms *(left)* would be barely visible without the reflected patches of sun on the wide columns. This demonstrates the value of a sunlit surface, seen in the distance from a darker space.

CAUTION
Before replacing part of a wall in your home with glass, check to make sure that the wall isn't acting as a fire wall.

▶ Take a tip from Scandinavian design traditions. Their interiors traditionally feature pale yellows, blues, greens, and greys, all containing a good deal of white, which bounces light across surfaces and gives rooms a luminous quality. Use shutters instead of heavy curtains at night; for daytime privacy, use sheer, open-weave fabrics, or muslins. During the day, sheer fabrics at windows catch whatever light is available and reflect or diffuse it to maximum effect.

▶ Light surfaces outside a window—such as pavements, decks, walls, and plants—play an important part in reflecting light into a room. A pool or garden pond outside a window can throw considerable amounts of light into a room—light that is vibrant and alive as the water moves and casts ripples on walls and ceilings.

▶ Light-colored foliage is also useful near a window. Ideally it should be deciduous so that the branches are bare in winter and do not shade precious daylight from the room. Remember that in a room facing away from the sun, the view of something sunlit outside can be nearly as good. Or, paint a wall a light color or plant silver or golden foliage that will catch the sun.

OUTSIDE SURFACES

The sun reflecting off this bright garden wall and the light green foliage outside make a significant contribution to the brightness and atmosphere of the room.

ARTISTIC SCREENING

These decorative pierced screens
(right) shade the room from
bright sun.

LIGHT SCREENS AND FILTERS

▶ In hot climates and on the sunniest days in colder ones,
you may need to filter and modify the light that streams
into your home. Look at the older building traditions of
North Africa, Moorish Spain, and Japan, where screens,
blinds, and shutters that catch and filter light cast
attractive patterns.

▶ Screens and slatted blinds have visual as well as
functional advantages, as they can be used for privacy and
to modify light during the day—when you are working at
a computer monitor, for example. When selecting a
screen or blind, remember that the nearer you are to it
the more you see through it, while a person across the
road will see considerably less. You can create an effective

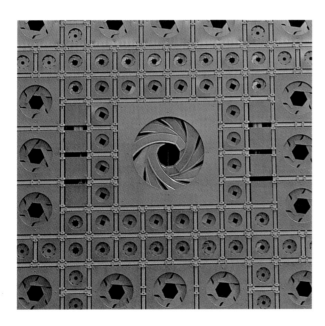

ARAB INSTITUTE, PARIS

A modern version of a traditional
screen *(above)* adjusts to let in
more or less daylight according to
exterior brightness.

BEFORE

Dark
corridor

AFTER

Skylight

Bathroom

Light-filled corridor

STAINED GLASS

An unappealing view of a parking lot has been transformed into an ever-changing burst of color by a specially commissioned stained glass, designed by artist Sarianne Durie *(above)*.

LATTICED SCREENS

Delicate wooden lattices *(left)* create a sense of enclosure and privacy in this room and add a rich pattern to the large panes of glass.

screen quite simply by putting slats or even thin shelves across the insides of windows.

▶ Pierced lattice screens with attractive patterns were developed in subtropical cities such as New Orleans. European designs included timber and iron, creating a richness similar to the traditions of Moorish and Persian architecture. The beauty of light-infused spaces created by the pierced marble screens and reflecting marble surfaces in the Islamic-Indian palaces at Fathepur Sikri, Agra, and Delhi and the exquisite pierced wooden shutters and screens in the Alhambra in southern Spain offer inspiration for dealing with excessive light in similar but more modest ways.

▶ Stained glass can introduce light of rich, strong colors. It can be used in homes but is relatively expensive and will reduce light levels considerably. Where light is not essential to the use of a room, such as in a hall or on a landing, stained glass can create dramatic and attractive effects. For example, a design that is predominantly yellow can give a sunny glow to north-facing spaces. (See page 191 for recommended reading on the use of stained glass in the home.)

PLANNING FOR LIGHT

Some lighting principles were used in planning the alterations of an urban house *(above)*. A first floor back extension had a bathroom with windows facing sideways, leaving a long, dark interior hallway leading to the back room. By inverting the original arrangement and placing the bathroom on the inside wall, the corridor benefited from the windows, while the bathroom was given a skylight. The corridor is now a sunny space filled with books, and acts as an extra room. The bathroom is flooded with light earlier in the day and needs no curtains for privacy.

ARTIFICIAL LIGHT

WHILE GOOD ARTIFICIAL ILLUMINATION is essential in the home, it consumes large amounts of electricity. Americans spend about 25 percent of their total electricity budget on lighting, which adds up to more than $37 billion per year. And most of that is spent on inefficient incandescent lighting. Energy-efficient bulbs—of which there are several different types—use as little as 20 percent of the energy consumed by incandescent bulbs, which reduces household energy bills and the amount of carbon dioxide emission from electricity generation. Typically, only 2 percent of electricity is generated from renewable sources. More than 60 percent comes from fossil fuel (oil, gas, and coal), and almost 33 percent is nuclear.

INCANDESCENT BULBS

Incandescent bulbs (also known as tungston bulbs), are the earliest form of lightbulbs. They work in a similar way to candles. Electricity is used to burn a tungsten filament in argon gas, giving off heat as well as light. These bulbs are extremely inefficient: No more than 15 percent of the energy consumed is given out as light, and the rest is heat. These bulbs last only about 1,000 hours because the metal filament burns away.

Incandescent light has a yellow cast, similar to the glow of late afternoon sunlight, which is why tungsten light is thought to be "warm." The light is directional, which gives shape and highlights texture.

COMPACT FLUORESCENT BULBS

Compact fluorescent bulbs work by heating an inert gas contained within a glass tube. They are four to five times more efficient than incandescent bulbs because once the gas has been energized, very little electricity is required to keep it glowing. The light emitted from an 11-watt fluorescent bulb, for example, is as bright as a 60-watt incandescent bulb. Because nothing burns, it gives off only a little heat and has a much longer life than an incandescent bulb—normally up to 10,000 hours.

Originally, fluorescent lights were made only in long tubes, but they are now universally available as compact fluorescent lamps, or CFLs, which can be installed in most light fixtures. Although CFLs are more expensive than incandescent bulbs, the combination of lower electricity consumption and a longer life means that CFLs become a better bargain after just 1,500 to 2,000 hours (the life of two incancescent bulbs).

CFL technology is improving all the time. The early problems that gave these bulbs a bad name (their shorter life when used in low temperatures or when switched on and off frequently; their slow start-up times) are being eliminated. Check these points with your retailer when buying bulbs, however, because not all manufacturers have resolved these difficulties. CFLs pose no risk of fire, and light fixtures designed for them are made in many different materials, including recycled paper and wood.

The color rendering of CFLs is very different from that of incandecent lights. The gas glows with colors high in the ultraviolet, blue, and green ranges, which gives the light its cold, bluish appearance—the reason why many people still prefer to use incandescent lights. But developments in the technology now allow a coating on the glass tubes of CFL lamps, creating different colors described as "warm white," "cool white," "daylight," or "full-spectrum." Daylight bulbs are considered healthier, as they more closely emulate the color range of natural daylight.

The light from fluorescent bulbs is also emitted over a large area, so it is more diffused and less directional than incandescent light. Older types of fluorescent lights oscillated at frequencies close to the brain's alpha waves and there were concerns that the flicker, even if unnoticeable, was dangerous. Frequencies are now much higher and these concerns are no longer valid.

Compact fluorescent lights provide the same brightness as incandescent bulbs with a lower wattage, thereby saving electricity. The following table compares the two:

INCANDESCENT	CFLs
60 watts	11 watts
75 watts	18 watts
100 watts	20 watts

TUNGSTEN HALOGEN BULBS

Low-voltage tungsten halogen bulbs burn tungsten elements in halogen gas, making them more than twice as efficient as conventional incandescent fixtures. The wattage can also generally be lower because all the light is concentrated on a smaller area, therefore increasing apparent brightness. Lower wattages also reduce electricity consumption. Tungsten halogen bulbs are small, with a strongly directional beam. They are available with beam angles ranging from 5 to 30 degrees and with warm and cool light characteristics, as well as in a range of strong colors. They have a life expectancy of 2,000 to 4,000 hours.

Because halogen bulbs are low voltage they require a transformer, which can be contained in the base of the fixture or located away from the light in a ceiling void or cupboard. Unlike other high-efficiency bulbs, tungsten halogen fixtures can be used with dimmers.

Low-voltage bulbs contain mercury vapor and halogens. When their use becomes more commonplace, disposal could become a problem since the bulbs could give off polluting emissions if not properly dealt with.

LIGHTING DESIGN

Lighting choices can make a radical difference in your home, affecting the appearance of rooms and objects, as well as the color, texture, mood, and atmosphere. The lowest possible energy consumption needs to be combined with the selection of the appropriate quality of light required—soft and diffused for general lighting, or brightly focused for tasks or display.

Lighting also comes with important safety considerations. Artificial lighting must meet a number of criteria: it must be safe for the task in hand—whether it is general illumination in corridors or stairs to avoid falls, or detailed task lighting for such activities as reading, sewing, or chopping vegetables. If you spend a lot of time working in a room that needs artificial light during the day, it is healthier to use full-spectrum lights that emulate daylight. These lights have been shown to counteract some of the effects of low winter light levels, which can cause Seasonal Affective Disorder, or SAD, in some people (see page 40).

Energy consumption can be drastically reduced by ensuring that lights are turned on only when needed.

SOFT LIGHTING

Focused downlighting provides an interesting pinpoint of light in this dim, cool interior. It augments the shaft of natural light from the double doors.

More and more installations are using "intelligent" technology—a light comes on when it senses the presence of people. Such sensors are usually used only in public places, or for external safety lights, but they could also be helpful in areas of the home such as hallways where lights might otherwise be left on all night.

LIGHTING TIPS

▶ Install as many low-energy lamps as possible.
▶ Design lighting for maximum task efficiency.
▶ Turn lights off when not needed.
▶ Use timers or motion sensors on external lights so that they are not left on all night.

HEAT

Indoors, our bodies are generally comfortable in a temperature range of about 64 to 80°F. But most people (except those living in extreme climates) experience natural external temperatures ranging from below freezing to 100°F or more. The need to create a comfortable living temperature from such external extremes explains why home heating consumes so much fuel and energy. Vast amounts of the earth's natural and irreplaceable resources are expended on home heating, with environmental consequences that are endangering our health and the future of our planet. Therefore, it is well worth thinking about how to minimize the heat input necessary to create the comfort we need.

The thermal performance of any home largely depends on its basic construction and orientation. Nevertheless, you can make a number of improvements that will significantly reduce fuel use and energy costs while creating a comfortable home:

▶ Turn down the heating in your home by a few degrees. You will save fuel and may feel better, too.

▶ Increase insulation to reduce energy demands.

▶ Seal your home so that as much energy as possible is retained, but make sure that it is also well ventilated (see page 74).

▶ Make use of free heat from the sun. This will also make your home attractive and bright (see page 66).

▶ Control heat so you use it where and when it's needed.

▶ Use the most efficient fuel, heat source, and method of heat distribution available.

KEEPING OUT THE COLD

Indoor spaces are protected from outside cold (or heat) by insulation, which works by trapping layers of still air to minimize heat transfer. This air can be held in a void, or in the spaces of a lightweight airy material. The best insulators are those that contain the most air. Of these, the safest are wood, wool, cotton, and shredded paper. Dense materials, such as stone, are the worst insulators.

A WARM HAVEN

This room's walls are lined with warm, unfinished softwood. The wood-burning stove has doors that can be closed and is set in a massive masonry structure that will store and radiate heat.

www. bonded logic . com — denim insulation (recycled)

INCREASING INSULATION

Walls of thick logs are used to make warm homes in cold climates. And thin layers of wooden paneling added to cold stone walls have long been used to increase warmth, as have rugs, weavings, and tapestries. For centuries, these materials have kept traditional homes warm and provided the opportunity for endless decorative invention—from the great wall-sized tapestries and oak panels in medieval castles to the simpler wall hangings and paneling in more modest homes today. (For more on wall coverings, see page 124.)

The effectiveness of wall hangings or paneling can be increased by adding an insulating backing. But don't pack the insulation material too tightly—always allow room for air movement to avoid problems with condensation.

Double-paned windows and insulating glass help to prevent heat from escaping through windows (see page 140).

Curtains, too, provide insulation and, as with wall hangings, the thicker the material the better. Sew weights into the hems so that the curtains stay in place and keep out drafts more efficiently. If you have radiators below your windows, keep curtains short so that they hang above the radiator, and place a shelf above the radiator to deflect heat into the room.

Curtains can also be hung over doors to keep drafts out. Insulated blinds help to limit cold radiation from windows at night. Internal shutters are another way to insulate windows. New shutters that fit in shutter boxes to match traditional woodwork are costly. But simpler shutters that can be hinged in the window frame or that slide on runners across the window are just as efficient. Adding insulation to shutters will make them even more effective.

WALL HANGINGS

These traditional hangings *(above)* around an old four-poster bed are an ideal way of keeping warmth in and cold drafts out. This idea can also be used to enclose areas of a room.

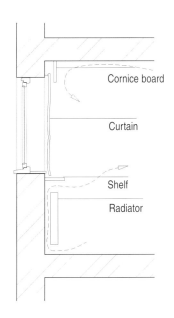

INCREASING EFFICIENCY

Two techniques for improving the efficiency of a radiator on an outside wall *(left)*. A shelf over the radiator pushes the air out into the room. A cornice board above the window prevents the warm air from circulating behind the curtains and onto the cold window.

Cornice board

Curtain

Shelf

Radiator

PREVENTING HEAT LOSS FROM FLOORS

Heat can also be lost through traditional raised ground floors that have air voids underneath. Air voids were a feature of a healthy form of construction designed to keep floor joists out of the damp earth and provide valuable ventilation to prevent or remove mold and dampness. For this reason, when insulating such floors to prevent heat loss into the air space, it is important to maintain ventilation from one side of the house to another.

If the space under the floor is large enough to crawl into, you can staple or pin insulation to the underside of the floor. Use a semi-rigid or batt-type insulation material, with a minimum thickness of 4 inches. If you cannot crawl under the floor, the only way to achieve good insulation is to lift the floorboards and drape netting over the floor beams (or joists) to contain the insulation. Alternatively,

DECORATIVE INSULATOR

Hung like a curtain over a large bedroom window, a beautiful kelim rug *(left)* acts as an effective insulator and also makes a striking, decorative feature in the room.

INTERNAL SHUTTERS

Heat-retaining shutters on this bathroom window *(above)* ensure that anyone using the bath is protected from cold drafts and has plenty of privacy. Wooden walls add warmth.

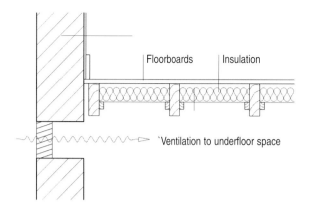

Floorboards | Insulation

Ventilation to underfloor space

RAISED FLOOR

Insulation between or under floor joists will increase the warmth of a raised floor *(left)*. It is essential to keep the air void well ventilated.

SOLAR GAIN

Large French doors allow plenty of sunlight to fall onto the dark, tiled floor of this room *(right)*. The floor absorbs solar heat during the day and radiates it back into the room in the cool of the evening.

use a rigid insulation and rest this on battens nailed to each side of the joists. If you are unable to do such extensive work, you can reduce the effect of drafty floorboards with a carpet laid over a thick pad. Do not make the mistake of laying plastic sheeting under the floor in the hope that this will prevent dampness—it will merely cause condensation. Dampness is best removed by ventilation.

Improve the insulation around your hot-water tank by using a properly designed insulating jacket. Even better, replace an old tank with one that has integral insulation. Ensure that your attic or crawl space has the maximum amount of insulation—generally no less than 6 inches. For more information on home insulation, see "Sources" on page 182.

SEALING IN WARMTH

Keep your home warm by minimizing the loss of warm air through drafts. There are two ways of doing this. First, seal gaps around doors and windows with rubber gaskets or nylon brush weather stripping; second, make a vestibule at each external door. These can make attractive entrance areas that are also useful for storing coats and shoes or displaying plants. When sealing your home, make sure that you create adequate ventilation to keep the internal air healthy—see page 74 for more on ventilation. The ideal is a warm house that stays at a reasonably constant temperature and has adequate and controllable levels of ventilation—a principle described by the Environmental Protection Agency (EPA) as "seal tight, ventilate right."

COLLECTING THE SUN'S WARMTH

Heavy, dark surfaces—concrete, tiles, or stone— absorb the sun's heat and radiate it back into the space when the temperature drops *(right)*.

FREE HEAT FROM THE SUN—SOLAR GAIN

The sun is the greatest source of energy we have and it is free. While using solar energy to its fullest requires comprehensive design of the building structure, you can gain significantly from relatively minor building work or decorating strategies. In most homes, the sun can provide up to about 10 percent of your warmth requirements, depending upon the building's orientation, setting, and construction.

Anyone with a window that lets in direct sunlight knows how much heat can be generated through the glass—this is known as solar gain. The challenge is to capture and store this warmth for as long as possible after the sun has set. Dark, heavy materials such as concrete, stone, or tiles absorb and store heat, then radiate it back into the space when the outside temperature drops. To make best use of this in rooms with a sunny orientation, use materials such as slate, dark ceramic tiles or even dark, painted concrete on floors, work surfaces, and other flat areas. The larger the area of glass, the more southerly the orientation, and the larger the absorbent surface, the greater the capacity to store and re-radiate heat. This idea must, of course, be

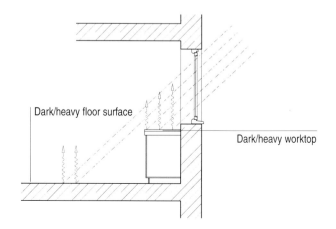

Dark/heavy floor surface

Dark/heavy worktop

Heavy stone walls and floors make efficient solar heat collectors in this sun-filled space *(left)*. The massive stones store the sun's warmth.

A centrally placed wood-burning stove radiates heat into this whole studio area *(right)*. It is an ideal form of heating in a large, high space.

▶ Method of heat distribution
▶ Flexibility of controls
▶ Type of fuel and burner

Heat is transmitted in three ways: by radiation, convection, and conduction. The first two play the greatest part in space heating. An ordinary cast-iron radiator illustrates the differences between these two forms of heat—the name "radiator" is, in fact, a misnomer because radiators emit only 30 percent of their heat by radiation and 70 percent by convection.

RADIANT HEAT

Radiant heat is the most efficient method of transmitting heat because it heats only the areas on which it is focused—the body or objects around it. Convection, on the other hand, must warm the air before we feel any heat. Which type is most practical and effective will depend on the nature of the space and its pattern of use. In normal domestic rooms, where the whole space is used and occupants want to move freely, it is more comfortable to heat the whole space by convection. But in larger, high spaces, or those used intermittently, such as workshops, studios, occasional play rooms, or stores, it is more efficient to use radiant heat that is focused on the area of activity, thus avoiding having to heat large volumes of air. Another advantage of radiant heat is that it is not lost through ven-

balanced with the desire to have light surfaces near windows to reflect light and increase brightness (see page 48).

With some construction work, it is possible to enlarge windows, add a bay, or make a sunporch, all of which collect solar gain. The larger the amount of external wall these devices can cover, the better, but bear in mind that any large windowed areas must be made of insulating glass. Many of the ideas discussed in the section on light (page 40) can be developed to provide solar warmth. Solar panels, of course, are the most effective way of making use of solar gain and can substantially reduce energy costs. (For more information see "Sources" on page 182.)

EFFICIENT HEAT DISTRIBUTION

In most existing houses, a heating system is needed at some times of year, even if you do increase insulation and make the best possible use of the sun's warmth. The efficiency of your heating system will depend upon the following:

Radiant heat is the most efficient form of heating because it heats quickly, and precisely where needed *(left)*. It is ideal in spaces with high ceilings.

tilation. However, some people find the sensation of radiant heat from above uncomfortable.

The simplest radiant devices are electric bar heaters, but these are dangerous. Safer and more practical, with a larger heat spread, are flat panels, which are heated either by electrical elements or by water pipes mounted behind them so that they are relatively unobtrusive. The larger the panel, the greater the heat output. One of the disadvantages of radiant panels is that they can be dangerously hot to touch, but the latest versions are panels with a relatively low temperature (77–113°F) that can be installed flush with the wall if you remove the plaster or drywall. They come either as mats with electrical coils or as thin, preformed radiators. Some can even be fitted behind plaster or drywall so that they cannot be seen. These inset panels radiate a gentle warmth and keep the wall warm. The disadvantage is that if you move out of their range you will not benefit from their heat, so the ambient air temperature should not be too low.

CONVECTED HEAT

Convected heat has a number of health disadvantages: It dries body tissues and membranes in our eyes, nose, throat, and skin, leading to irritations and making us susceptible to colds. This is one of the factors cited for winter cold syndromes. Convected air also stirs up dust, exacerbates odors, and has a slower warm-up time.

Convection heaters work by heating air as it passes over hot surfaces. Thus, the larger the surface area, the larger the heat output. Fins on the back of a radiator increase the

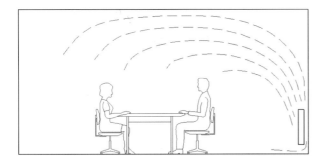

CONVECTED HEAT
Convected heat relies on air passing over a hot surface: A space will become warm only when the whole volume of air is heated.

surface area without increasing the width and height. Also available are very compact radiators that are enclosed and contain a fan that draws air in from near the floor and forces it up over the hot fins. Known as "convector heaters," these are small and efficient—but you should avoid them because the fans consume electricity, stir up dust, and require maintenance.

Whatever form of heating you choose, be sure to locate heat vents or radiators carefully and consider the following points:
▶ Add spacer blocks behind radiators to increase the air movement.
▶ Avoid obstructing radiators, heat vents, or baseboard units with furniture or curtains. Place a shelf above any radiators under windows so that the air moves out into the room instead of rising behind curtains or blinds.

INSULATION
This room constructed from logs is
well insulated and needs no other
adornment.

▶ Distribute heat evenly by using several small radiators or heaters rather than a single large one.

▶ Avoid placing radiators on outside walls, where some of the heat will radiate to the outside, unless you take precautions. If a radiator has to be on an outside wall, place as much insulation behind it as possible and add a reflective membrane.

CONTROLLING HEAT

The approach of simply letting a furnace run in the winter months, pumping heat into the whole house, is terribly inefficient; try to avoid this. Heating can be operated by a simple on-off switch, a preset timer, or, most efficiently, with a thermostatic control that allows you to adjust the temperature in each space or zone. Retrofitting your current system to be controllable by zones lets you adjust heat for individ-

ual comfort and patterns of use, and reflects weather conditions or indoor heat-generating activities such as cooking. For even greater efficiency, arrange any new installation so that areas of the house with different uses—such as bedrooms and living rooms—are on separate heating circuits, allowing them to operate at different times and heat levels.

Remember, too, that your sense of comfort depends on the amount of ventilation available, the activities you're engaged in, and your personal metabolism. The greater the amount of control you have over the heating in your home, the easier it is to accommodate these factors and ensure minimum waste and maximum comfort.

BACKGROUND HEAT

Another way of heating efficiently is to keep the home at a good background temperature. You can then up the heat in individual rooms, depending upon weather conditions, and introduce high heat only where and when it is needed. This works particularly well in stone or brick houses which, if left unheated at night or for parts of the day, can become very cold and require large amounts of energy to bring them up to a reasonable temperature. A background heat of about 59°F will mean that on many days in the winter months only a small boost of extra heat is required to make the house comfortable. In cold climates, background heat is also important for protecting your house from frost and condensation damage.

Underfloor heating, using either electrical cables or hot-water pipes, is an ideal form of background heating for homes with solid concrete floors covered with stone or tiles. Systems using hot water pipes beneath wood floors are also an option. Underfloor heating radiates a general background heat into the space and makes cold floors comfortable to walk on. Although expensive to install, this form of heating is efficient for two reasons. First, it warms the feet, often the coldest part of the body, which allows the general room temperature to be a few degrees lower than normal. Second, the heavy mass of a solid floor allows intermittent heat input because the floor will store warmth and remain at a relatively stable temperature. Pipes and cables need to be embedded in a sand and cement layer (screed) that is at least 3 inches thick. If you do not have enough depth in the floor for cables or pipes, a system that uses thin mats containing slender cables is an option. These mats won't provide full heating but will simply take the chill out of the stone.

WOOD-BURNING STOVES

Stoves make any home look warm and cozy and are an ideal way of boosting background heat. Wood is a renewable resource, but wood-burning stoves are only environmentally sound if they are efficient, high-temperature models, (called clean-burn or double-circulation burners) that reduce smoke emissions and particulates. Wood-burning stoves can use low-grade timber and woodland industry waste and thinnings, as well as pellets made from waste. If you use pellets, check their content to be sure that they are safe. Always burn dry wood—wet wood emits smoke.

Wood-burning stoves are also useful for providing the small amount of heat needed in spring and autumn, when external temperatures are a bit chilly, but heating the whole house is unwarranted. You can achieve greater efficiency by linking a wood-burning stove with a backboiler to one or two radiators in places that particularly need heating, such as the bathroom. In most temperate areas, a fire burning in a living area will give background heat that should shorten the period when central heating, fired by fossil fuel, is needed throughout the home. Dual installations, where radiators can be served by either the backboiler or the central heating furnace, are ideal, but they can be expensive and require careful designing by a qualified engineer.

The heavier the stove—and particularly the more central and massive the chimney—the more efficient it will be because the structure as well as the stove will store and radiate heat into the house. This is the principle behind the massive stoves used in northern Europe and Scandinavia.

When choosing a wood-burning stove, look for:
▶ Solid construction
▶ Closed-door type with a tight door seal

▶ Recirculating air chambers to maximize the burn-out of emissions
▶ Ease of loading for safety

Ensure that any wood-burning stove is set up correctly by a qualified installer. And have your chimney swept at the end of every winter to avoid the risk of chimney fires as a result of the build-up of soot in the chimney.

FUEL AND HEAT SOURCES

The efficiency of your heating system will depend on the type of fuel available and whether the heat is distributed by a central furnace or local room heaters. In terms of environmental impact, fuels can be rated in order of preference, as follows:

1. Renewable energy from sun, wind, or heat pumps
2. Burning of landfill gas emissions, sewage gas, and/or agricultural waste*
3. Wood, provided it is burned at sufficiently high temperatures
4. Natural gas
5. Oil and liquid petroleum gas
6. Coals and anthracites
7. Smokeless fuels
8. Electricity generated from fossil fuels
  *Burning waste is simply a way of dealing with an environmental problem, and incineration must be efficient and clean to avoid the production of polluting emissions and particulates.

Most people in existing homes will have a limited variety of fuels to choose from, and your choice will also be governed by reliability of supply. Of the nonrenewable fuels, natural gas should be the first choice because it converts most efficiently into heat with the minimum amount of polluting emissions.

The type of heating system you install will depend upon your choice of fuel. The following are broad but generally accepted orders of efficiency for the conversion of different fuels into heat. The figures show how important furnace efficiency is if we are to reduce fossil fuel use.

GAS

▶ Condensing furnace: 80–85 percent*
▶ Forced hot-air furnace: 65–70 percent
▶ Gas furnace with natural convection flue: 50–65 percent (depends upon age)

  *While gas condensing furnaces are generally about 25 percent more expensive, they save sufficient gas to pay for themselves during their lifetime.

SOLID FUEL (WOOD, ANTHRACITE COAL)

▶ Automatic feed furnace: 65 percent
▶ Closed space heater: 60 percent
▶ Open fire in grate: 30–35 percent

ELECTRICITY*

▶ Boiler, panels, and convector heaters: 100 percent
▶ Fan-assisted space heaters: 80 percent
▶ Off-peak storage heaters: 75 percent

  *It is important to note that while electric room heaters are efficient, environmental damage occurs when making electricity from fossil fuel. Taking this into account, the efficiency of electric space heating is estimated at only about 25 percent of natural gas efficiency.

AIR AND VENTILATION

L IKE SUNSHINE AND CLEAN WATER, fresh air is vital for healthy body processes, and access to it has been taken as a right. Today, we tend to forget its importance and have almost managed to eliminate fresh air from our lives.

We need fresh air in our homes, not only for the body's metabolic functions but also to remove mold spores and viruses from the home and prevent the accumulation of chemical offgassing, dust, and uncombusted gases from home appliances. In addition, it cools us when interiors become too warm.

The extent of the harm that chemicals and dust do to indoor air quality is only just beginning to be understood. So far, statistics for health in workplaces are more readily available than for health in homes. In one survey of 223 buildings where occupants complained of a variety of health problems, inadequate fresh air occurred in 65 percent and poor distribution of air in 46 percent.

The better the **ventilation,** the **healthier** the **home**

Poor indoor air is also a result of dust particles. The problem is that the finer the particles, the less we are aware of them, but the more potential they have to harm our lungs. In addition, unventilated moist air encourages mold spores and bacterial growth—all of which affect our lungs and can potentially lead to respiratory diseases. To create a healthy home, try to eliminate the majority of pollutants at their source by avoiding materials that off-gas unwanted chemicals. But the need to replenish fresh air in your home regularly will always remain: The better the ventilation, the healthier the home.

CHANGING THE AIR

The amount of fresh air needed in any space for any given activity is expressed as the number of air changes per hour—this means the number of times the entire volume of air in a space is completely replaced with fresh air. The World Health Organization (WHO) recommends that in living areas, when people are generally doing routine domestic tasks or relaxing, the air should be changed 0.5 times per hour—in other words, a complete air change every 2 hours. In an old "leaky" house this need would be met automatically without any other actions. It has been estimated that loose-fitting windows, doors, and open chimneys give a background air-change rate of 0.7 per hour. Recommended change rates for bedrooms are 1.3 times per hour, and for bathrooms, kitchens, or any areas where people are very active, they rise to 6 changes per hour. In rooms where people are smoking, as many as 10 to 15 air changes per hour are recommended.

Background air-change rates have been radically reduced in modern, tightly sealed homes, making the need for proper ventilation even more pressing. In Canada, for instance, building regulations now require buildings to be sealed so that they are almost "air-leak free," permitting only 0.1 air change per hour, just one-fifteenth of the recommended air change rate.

CREATING PROPER VENTILATION

While outside air is often less clean than we might wish, it can still be up to ten times cleaner than indoor air. So unless you suffer from sensitivities to particular external pollutants that need filtering out, you should ventilate

A FLEXIBLE DESIGN

This window arrangement offers flexibility and control. The under-sill panel is hinged to act as a door in summer. Shutters provide light-reflecting panels by day and insulation at night.

with external air rather than using air conditioning. Air conditioners harm the environment by their energy consumption, the heat they emit to the atmosphere, and their use of polluting refrigerant gases. Simpler passive techniques for ventilation and cooling have been used in buildings for centuries. They have no environmental impact, are safe to use, and cost nothing.

A number of principles govern air movement in a building, and these are useful to bear in mind when considering ventilation methods.

▶ Unequal air pressure exists on different sides of a building, which can create air flow.

▶ Air inlet and exit spots are necessary for air movement.

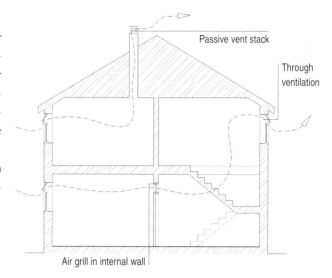

Passive vent stack

Through ventilation

Air grill in internal wall

PASSIVE VENTILATION

Openings positioned at high and low levels in a house allow the passage of air and create natural air movement without the need for mechanical fans or other devices *(above)*. Outlets at the roof level are particularly effective.

▶ Air movement outside a building increases with the building's height.

▶ Warm air rises, while cold air falls—the "stack effect."

▶ Polluted air tends to rise.

▶ Evaporation cools a surface.

There are many ways to create good ventilation. Those most suitable for your home depend on factors such as the way it is built, its orientation, and the size of the windows.

The best way to ensure good air flow through a home is to have air entry and exit points (preferably at high levels) on different sides of the building, with clear routes for the air to travel between them. Except on the stillest days, the pressure difference on opposite sides of a building will draw air from one side through to the other. This applies to individual rooms as well as entire dwellings. It is more efficient to have two small openings on opposite sides of a room than to have one window wide open.

Windows and skylights can be fitted with devices that allow a tiny opening to admit a trickle of air while avoiding a draft. There are two forms—one is a night-vent han-

VENTILATION AND SHADE

A decorative window grill allows constant ventilation and provides shade. This simple room *(left)* needs no other decorative features.

EXTERIOR SHUTTERS
Traditional louvered shutters *(right)*
shield a room from the sun while
allowing plenty of air movement.

EXTERIOR SHUTTERS
Traditional louvered shutters *(right)*
shield a room from the sun while
allowing plenty of air movement.

dle that keeps the window secure while slightly ajar. The other is a slot ventilator that can be fitted into a window frame. This thin channel has an open-closed slide position and provides a secure way of ventilating a room at night. It can be added to existing windows, provided that their frames are thick enough, or it can be fitted at the top of the glass. Good-quality, modern windows come already fitted with night-vents or slot ventilators.

AIRBRICKS AND SHUTTERS

Wall-mounted airbricks (openings as small as the size of a single brick) are an excellent way to create natural ventilation. Unlike traditional airbricks that are open permanently, wall-mounted airbricks can be fitted with sliding or hinged covers to control air flow. They can be located on outside or inside walls to allow cross-ventilation. In hot climates, large vent openings above doors or high up on walls can be used to allow plenty of air movement through a room, and they are not difficult to install. Another way of encouraging air circulation without loss of warmth is to locate airbricks behind radiators so that incoming air is heated rather than creating cold drafts. Controllable airbricks should be used in this situation.

Windows can be fitted with shutters, grills, and trellises to allow ventilation while creating privacy and security. Shutters with hinged flaps are particularly effective. They make it possible to vary how much of the screen is open. In traditional buildings, screens and shutters are made in a wide variety of materials and patterns and can be attractive architectual features. In Spain, for example, screens and shutters made of local wood were pierced with geometric shapes and patterns, illuminating the cool, dark interiors with pinpoints of light like the night sky. Emperors in India

INTERIOR SHUTTERS
Half-shutters *(right)* provide privacy while the window is open for ventilation, while light streams in through the upper window.

A COOLING POOL
Open ventilation screens allow in
cool, moist air *(left)*—thanks to the
indoor pool, a simple form of natural
air conditioning.

A SHADY PORCH
A porch *(right)* provides a cool,
shady spot to enjoy the open air out
of direct sunlight. It also shades the
house walls from the hot sun.

adorned their palaces with heavy stone screens carved with
elaborate patterns which both provided ventilation and
absorbed the sun's heat (see page 54). These examples can
inspire us to make practical devices that are also decorative.

ROOF VENTILATORS AND VENT STACKS

Roof ventilators exploit the stack effect to release rising
hot air. This is why old chimneys were so effective at providing ventilation—and so drafty. You can create natural
ventilation with the stack effect by using skylights that
open, small flue-outlet pipes through the roof with ceiling
grills, or airbricks placed high up on walls. Locate the
openings in a central space, such as a stairwell or central
living room, and add small vents in internal walls to inter-
connecting rooms. Air will be drawn in at low level and
drawn out at a high level.

The principles of passive vent stacks have long been used
in simple devices such as wind scoops, so common in the
Middle East. With these as inspiration, a number of passive
ventilation stack devices have been developed to ventilate
internal rooms, particularly bathrooms, and to create natural ventilation throughout a home. They are essentially
pipes that run vertically to vent at the top of a building, and
rely on the air movement at a high level to draw air up and
out of the room. Specially shaped cowls assist the upward
draw of air—the cowls can be fitted with small low-
energy fans to increase efficiency where necessary. In order
to work properly, these devices also require air coming into
the house through any of the methods described above.
Passive air inlet vents are available that respond to indoor
humidity and open or close automatically.

ROOFTOP WIND CATCHERS
Traditional ventilation devices, these
wind catchers at the tops of buildings
in Yemen *(left)* have become
attractive architectural features.

Passive ventilation systems are now accepted by some environmental health departments as alternatives to electric exhaust fans in bathrooms and kitchens. In winter, it is more cost-effective to have a continuous, slow-running small electric fan on a passive ventilation stack in a kitchen than to open windows to let out large amounts of expensively heated air. Installation in a single story or the upper floors of multistory buildings is relatively easy: The disruption involved in routing a system through two floors will depend on the layout of your home. Passive vent stacks can often be taken through cupboards, but you'll need to cut holes in floors and ceilings to accommodate them. Wrap the pipe in sound-reducing material to avoid creating noise paths between rooms.

COOLING

Air movement across the body causes evaporation from the skin, which lowers body temperature. The greater the amount of ventilation (the faster the air movement) in a room, the cooler you can stay. This is much easier in hot climates, where outside air brought into the building does not cause cold drafts. In cooler climates, the problem is trickier because you may want to cool down without losing expensively heated air, so you need to strike a balance between air movement and heat loss.

Cooling by mechanical means can be achieved in two ways: fan-assisted air movement, which moves ambient air over the body, or air conditioning, which cools the air and then distributes it. If air flow is inadequate, fan-assisted air movement is environmentally much safer to use than air conditioning, which is so damaging (as described on page 74). Ceiling fans can create comfort by assisting air movement but, because they consume electricity, they should be considered only if passive ventilation techniques are not sufficient. While a fan obviously creates cooling air movement, its effectiveness in replenishing air depends largely on its relationship with open windows.

A traditional method of cooling in hot climates combines the cooling characteristic of evaporation with the stack effect. Water is placed in a porous jar at the base of a chimney or vertical vent stack. As hot air rises up the chimney and over the jar, it evaporates the water, lowering the temperature of both the water and the vessel. More air

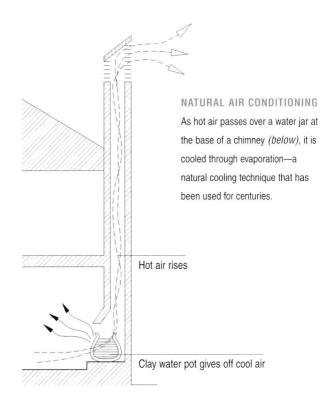

OPEN AIR
The ultimate in fresh air—one wall of this bedroom *(right)* can be opened up, breaking down the distinction between indoor and outdoor spaces.

NATURAL AIR CONDITIONING
As hot air passes over a water jar at the base of a chimney *(below)*, it is cooled through evaporation—a natural cooling technique that has been used for centuries.

Hot air rises

Clay water pot gives off cool air

is then drawn into the chimney from below, constantly moving air through the dwelling. In effect, it's natural air conditioning. Even if you don't have a chimney, you can place a porous earthenware water container under an open window for a similar effect. The more porous the vessel the better, so that the surface of the jar itself has a cooling effect in the space. An indoor pool is a more elaborate solution, which will not only cool the air but also create a refreshing atmosphere.

BREATHING BUILDINGS

Another factor in determining healthy indoor air quality is the extent to which buildings can dissipate water vapor and bioeffluents through their construction. This was usually the case in older buildings made from natural vapor-permeable materials. Many modern building materials are impermeable and therefore seal in moisture-laden air, which contributes to dampness, mold growth, and spores.

Whenever weather permits, open your windows
to allow plenty of fresh air into rooms and stop the
build-up of stale air *(below)*.

These, in turn, can cause respiratory problems. We see this
effect regularly when warm, steamy bathroom or kitchen
air condenses on tiled or high-gloss painted walls. What we
don't realize is that this process is taking place in all our
spaces most of the time, but even if the walls are only partially permeable they still tend to absorb much of the
moisture that is generated.

Research in building construction, particularly in
Germany and California, is showing that buildings are
complex systems that react with people and the environment in a symbiotic, almost biological way. This theory,
known as *Bau-biologie* (German for "building biology"),
demonstrates that buildings need to be constructed so they
are flexible and responsive to climate, air, and moisture.
Breathing buildings help create good indoor air quality.

While as homeowners we cannot change the construction of our buildings, we can help to make our buildings
more permeable and responsive by our decorating choices. Materials suitable for breathing walls are lime and mud
plasters (normal gypsum plasters are partially permeable),
timber, cork and most fiberboards, fabrics, linoleum, and
low-fired, unglazed tiles.

HIGH WINDOWS
In hot climates, rooms are cooled by openings
that maximize drafts. These high windows *(left)*
let out rising hot air and generate cooling currents.

To summarize, the following guidelines will help you achieve healthy ventilation for your home.

DO:
▶ Ensure air-change level is suited to the use of the room.
▶ Arrange ventilation openings, such as windows and vents, to assist drafts.
▶ Fit night-vent handles or slot-ventilators on windows.
▶ Use passive rather than energy-consuming techniques.
▶ Install passive-vent stacks.
▶ Decorate walls with vapor-permeable paints and papers.
▶ On walls that require water-resistant materials, use linoleum, oily timber such as cedar, or tiles only on areas that get wet.

DON'T:
▶ Seal your home tightly without ventilating it.
▶ Line walls with plastic materials.
▶ Use wall-sealing paints.
▶ Use an air-conditioning system.

VENTILATION FOR RADON GAS
Radon gas occurs naturally in the ground in some areas—usually where the underlying rock is granite. The gas rises and is dispersed naturally unless it becomes trapped in sealed areas beneath a building and then leaks through the floor. Radon has a very short life when mixed with sufficient air. Protective measures, therefore, involve underfloor ventilation, which dilutes and disperses the gas. Full protective measures can be achieved only during construction, but in areas where radon is particularly high, partial measures to reduce its impact are recommended in existing buildings. These include installing continuous fans to vent underfloor spaces and wall cavities. The work should be carried out under the guidance of your local building inspector, who should have maps indicating land areas where this problem exists. Radon-testing services are now widely available in most areas.

SOUND

Sound—whether music or noise—surrounds us in a way that is more all-embracing than any other sensory stimulation. People often describe a sound as "going right through you," and sounds have extraordinary power to move us. Unwanted sound—which is perhaps the best definition of noise—can affect us to such a degree as to cause stress and even illness. The power of sound may be due to the fact that sound is caused by the vibration of air waves, which resonate with our bodily vibrations. Noise increases the rate of heartbeat, while silence can slow it down and induce relaxation. A safe and healthy home, therefore, needs to be a quiet home.

One reason why noise causes such significant levels of stress is because we can seldom control its source. We can turn away from things we don't want to see or move to avoid touching something, but with noise, someone somewhere else is in control. These stress-inducing factors are in addition to the simple physical damage that can be caused by prolonged exposure to noise.

The act of hearing involves two aspects of sound—the range of low to high sounds, referred to as frequency (measured in cycles per second), and the level of loudness (measured in decibels). Someone with good hearing will hear sounds from a low (bass) frequency of 20 cycles per second up to very high-frequency sounds of 20,000 cycles per second, regardless of whether the sound is loud or soft. This difference is important when dealing with noise because low-frequency sounds are much more difficult to prevent than high-level sounds. That is why when noise comes through a wall, we hear many more low-level bass notes than the higher notes of speech or music.

COMFORTABLE ACOUSTICS
This room has comfortable, soft acoustics because its variously angled surfaces, textured floor, and textured ceiling absorb and deaden internal noise.

SOUND, HEARING, AND DANGEROUS NOISE

The relationship between our ability to hear a sound and its loudness level (regardless of whether it is high or low frequency) is not constant: Each 1-decibel increase in measured sound levels reflects an increase in the intensity (or power) of sound by a factor of ten. Putting this simply, someone listening to the faint sound of a single bird singing in a quiet environment will be listening to a sound that would measure close to 0 decibels, which is considered the lowest threshold of hearing. A person with poor hearing who cannot hear sound below 40 decibels but wants to hear birdsong will need to listen not to 40 birds but to 10,000 birds, and someone who cannot hear below 50 decibels will need to be sung to by 100,000 birds!

To give an idea of what these sound levels mean in everyday terms, a quiet rural area will have a background noise level of 20 to 30 decibels, a residential side road during the day might measure about 45 decibels, a reasonably quiet office with quiet conversation will have a background level of 60 decibels, while busy offices can be on the level of 70 to 80 decibels. Noisy power tools and heavy traffic measure 80 to 100 decibels, while a loud rock concert measured within 15 yards of the speakers might be as much as 110 to 120 decibels.

Damage to hearing is caused by both the level of sound and length of exposure. Thus, recommendations for safe sound levels specify both loudness level and period of exposure. Background noise of up to about 60 decibels should cause no disturbance, while 80 decibels is considered the maximum that is safe for any extended period of time. Exposure limits are recommended to be eight hours for levels up to 85 decibels, 2 hours for up to 95 decibels and 15 minutes for anything around 110 decibels. Above this, there is rapid hearing loss. The idea that hearing loss caused by noise is only temporary is a myth. Excessive noise exposure damages sensory cells in the ear, which do not regenerate or repair. Unlike many illnesses, hearing loss is not reversible.

WAYS THAT NOISE IS TRANSMITTED

There are two types of sound: airborne, and impact (or structure-borne). Airborne sound is any sound that travels to the ear through the air. Typically, this includes speech, most music, and traffic noise. Sound travels through the air in waves, so the only satisfactory way of reducing the transmission of airborne sound is to block the paths of sound waves.

Impact sound is generated by the impact of something heavy striking a surface, causing the sound to travel along or through the material. Footsteps on the floor of the room above or a neighbor banging on a shared wall are typical impact sounds. Buildings with concrete floors or frames are much more susceptible to transmitting impact noise because the structure is continuous and sound can travel through the structure. For example, when pipes at one end of a building are hammered, the sound travels to the other end.

For an acoustically healthy home, there are a number of actions that you can take:

▶ Reduce both airborne and impact noise coming into the home.

▶ Create a comfortable acoustic environment.

▶ Plan your home to reduce internal noise.

REDUCING AIRBORNE NOISE

Noise travels through the weakest link in any structure. So the soundproofing afforded by a heavy wall counts for little if a window is left open. When planning to reduce noise, we need to look not only at the mass of the wall but also at the design of potential noise paths, such as windows, doors, and holes through walls for pipes or chimneys. Simple ways of limiting the amount of noise coming into your home include:

▶ Seal all noise paths, or make them as difficult for soundwaves to pass through as possible.

▶ Hang heavy curtains at your windows, or consider installing wooden shutters.

▶ Outside your home, add soft landscaping, which reduces the amount of sound that can travel up into the windows. Physical barriers, such as walls, fences, and earth berms, deflect traffic noise upward and away from lower windows and garden areas.

▶ Add double glazing or, better still, secondary windows. Sound is weakened by the air gap between the panes of glass; the larger the air gap, the better the sound reduction. Line the jambs between the inner and outer

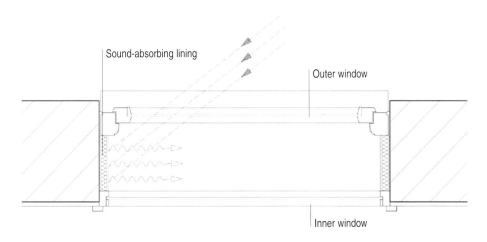

Sound-absorbing lining

Outer window

Inner window

DOUBLE WINDOWS
Sound insulation is created by an air space between the inner and outer windows *(left)*. The sill, jambs, and head between the windows should be lined with sound-absorbing material.

panes in order to absorb some of the sound before it is transmitted through the inner pane.

NOISE REDUCTION WITH GLASS AND WINDOWS

Constant traffic noise can be a serious and debilitating problem, causing stress and sleep deprivation. The table below shows the typical levels of traffic noise from different sorts of roads and the reduction required to make comfortable sound conditions in living rooms and bedrooms. It also shows ways of achieving these reductions by the use of different types of glass and windows. Figures are given in dbA—a measurement of noise disturbance—rather than pure sound levels.

The noise-reduction measures that are outlined in the table might be costly. If you suffer from excessive traffic noise, consult an architectural or engineering firm that specializes in noise remediation. A glass manufacturer will also be able to help you. (For more information on different types of glass, such as laminated and audio-reducing, see page 140.)

NOISE REDUCTION (measured in dbA) ACHIEVED BY DIFFERENT TYPES OF GLASS

traffic noise measured in dbA	living room recommended level 40-45 dbA	bedroom recommended level 30-40 dbA
residential road 60 dbA	**20–15 reduction in dbA** USING SINGLE GLAZING ¼-inch float (ordinary glass)	**30–20 reduction in dbA** USING SINGLE GLAZING ¼-inch laminated glass
major road 70 dbA	**30–25 reduction in dbA** USING SINGLE GLAZING ⁵⁄₁₆-inch sound-reducing glass	**40–30 reduction in dbA** USING DOUBLE GLAZING ½-inch and ½-inch sound-reducing glass
city street 75 dbA	**35–30 reduction in dbA** USING DOUBLE GLAZING ⁵⁄₁₆-inch sound-reducing glass and ⅜-inch float	**45–35 reduction in dbA** USING DOUBLE WINDOWS ¼-inch float, 4-inch space, ¼-inch float
highway 80 dbA	**40–35 reduction in dbA** USING DOUBLE WINDOWS ¼-inch float, 6-inch space, ¼-inch float	**50–40 reduction in dbA** USING DOUBLE WINDOWS ⅜-inch float, 8-inch space, ¼-inch float

NOISE REDUCTION THROUGH WALLS

The best way to prevent noise from transferring through walls is to make the walls heavier by, for example, adding a layer of drywall, heavy plywood, or ceramic tiles. The lower the frequency of the noise, the heavier the wall has to be if it is to have any effect in reducing it. Adding sound-absorbent materials also helps, particularly with higher-frequency sounds such as high-pitched music and the upper levels of speech.

I dealt successfully with the problem of noise coming through walls in a 19th-century row house. The occupants were suffering from loud noise coming through a shared wall from the next-door neighbors, and all their appeals for quiet were ignored. The solution was a combination of mass and absorption. The wall was lined with four layers of ½-inch drywall, which was nailed to battens. The space between the battens was filled with sound-insulating batts, which are much denser than heat-insulating batts. To ensure that the installation covered all potential weak spots, including voids in the ceiling and floor structure, we lifted floorboards and cut into the ceiling so that the new insulaton extended into and across all of the voids.

I had warned the client that it would be impossible to predict the extent of sound reduction because sound traveling through structures, particularly when they are old, relies on so many factors. After the alterations, there were still occasional low-frequency rumbles, but the noises were so much fainter and less frequent that the family was relieved of sound-induced stress.

It is also possible to increase the mass of a floor in a number of ways, most commonly by adding sound-insulating batts or sand within the structure. Sound-reducing mats and underlays are available from specialty flooring or carpet suppliers and are particularly effective for reducing impact noise.

CAUTION

Before increasing the load on any structure by adding mass, first check with a structural engineer or your local building inspector to ensure the existing structure can support the extra weight.

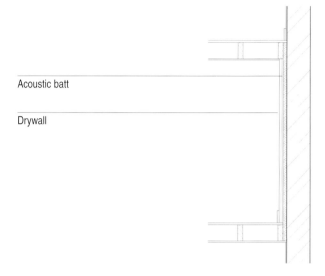

Acoustic batt

Drywall

INCREASING SOUND REDUCTION

To improve the sound-reducing performance of a wall, add drywall to increase weight and stop low-frequency noise. Add acoustic batt to absorb high-frequency sound *(above)*.

HARSH ACOUSTICS

The smooth, hard surfaces and lack of soft furnishings in this sophisticated minimalist dining room *(left)* create harsh, echoey acoustics.

SOFT ACOUSTICS

The wooden ceiling and textured surfaces in this room *(above)* are excellent sound absorbers. The low-energy lights give a warm glow.

REDUCING IMPACT NOISE

A hard surface transmits noise by acting like a drum. To prevent noise transmission, the source of the impact noise must be isolated from the relevant surface. For example, a washing machine mounted on an absorbent surface creates far less noise than one placed on a hard surface. Avoid acoustically absorbent materials made of foamed plastics and use cork, rubber, or felt instead. Carpet is also a useful sound absorber, but it will tend to depress over time and lose its value. You can also use special antivibration mounting blocks for machinery such as furnace pumps.

Kitchens and bathroom walls can generate noise because of the many hard surfaces they contain. Be aware of this when locating a sink, toilet, or water tanks or pipes—the vibrations of running water will transmit noise into an adjacent room. If such fixtures must be located against an

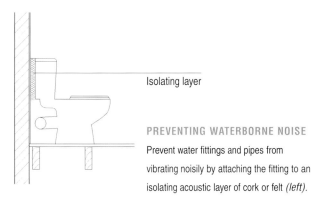

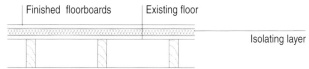

PREVENTING WATERBORNE NOISE
Prevent water fittings and pipes from vibrating noisily by attaching the fitting to an isolating acoustic layer of cork or felt *(left)*.

FLOATING FLOOR
Prevent the noise of footfalls from overhead by laying a rigid floor on an isolating layer such as cork *(above)*.

SOFT CEILING
A ceiling lined with soft, sound-absorbent grass makes this sleeping nook *(right)* cozy and quiet.

internal wall, they can be isolated with a resilient layer of cork or rubber. Or if you are installing tile behind a sink, isolate the tiles by gluing plywood and a soft separating layer to the wall. Then attach the tiles or waterproof splashback to the board. The board must be glued—screw inserts create hard paths for sound transmission.

Noise in pipes can often be prevented by minor amendments to the pipework installation. Changes need to be carried out by a plumber, who will identify solutions to what could be a variety of problems, such as water hammers, restricted pipes, or air locks. Noise transmitted by pipes commonly occurs when they pass through holes that are too tight, thereby transmitting the vibrations into the structure. Make holes larger, then seal them with a flexible caulking compound.

An all-too-common problem is noise transmitted from the floor of one apartment to the rooms below. Airborne noise can be dealt with by making the ceiling heavier, but the real difficulties come if the apartment above yours has hard floors. The best solution is for your upstairs neighbors to install a resilient layer, such as carpet with good quality padding. In bathrooms or kitchens where carpet is not practical, linoleum or rubber flooring can be laid over a thin resilient underlay for a similar effect. Resilient-backed flooring tends to be vinyl, so if you plan to install such a floor, seek the few products on the market that are made with low VOCs or petrochemical content.

A more difficult and expensive solution is to install a "floating floor," which isolates a hard wooden floor from the main floor structure by a continuous resilient layer. The resulting change of level will also require changes to doors and thresholds.

CREATING ACOUSTIC COMFORT

It is impossible to avoid sound being generated within the home, but whether this causes any disturbance is dependent upon the acoustic quality of a space.

Hard surfaces such as stone, tiles, polished wood, and plain plastered walls reflect noise and can create a very harsh acoustic environment. The extent of any problems will depend upon individual noise tolerance and hearing, as well as how the space is used. An empty room with many hard surfaces may be fine when occupied by a couple talking, but if that space is filled with people and loud music, a very different and uncomfortable sound atmosphere is created. This is because sounds bounce off hard surfaces in all directions at the same time, sending the ear a mass of random mixed sounds. The same situation in a room full of soft furnishings will be far less disturbing, even though the level of sound generated may be much the same.

As sound is reflected from all surfaces in a room, it is not particularly important where you locate hard and soft surfaces. If you want to retain a beautiful polished wood or stone floor, compensate by adding full-length curtains and lots of soft furniture and cushions. Alternatively, try putting up some wall hangings or even something soft on the ceiling to absorb some of the sound.

If you have a minimalist interior, free from soft furnishings, but you want a quieter space, you can install walls or ceilings with a backing of acoustic absorbent material, similar to that used in concert halls. The wall or ceiling material is pierced, allowing sound to travel through to the soft backing, which absorbs the sound and avoids echoes.

LOWERED CEILING

In this room *(left)*, a lowered ceiling, consisting of textured, sound-absorbing panels, counteracts the resonant qualities of the hard floor and walls.

WALL OF WARDROBES

A wall lined with storage units *(below)* makes a highly effective acoustic barrier to sound coming from neighboring rooms or buildings.

PLANNING TO AVOID NOISE

If you can, minimize noise disturbance within the home by arranging the spaces so that noisy and quiet areas do not impinge on each other. For example, avoid playrooms or TV rooms immediately adjacent to bedrooms. If your home offers no flexibility, consider using built-in furniture as a noise buffer. Line a wall between rooms that need sound separation with wardrobes or wall storage units. The more solid they are, the better, and they should cover the whole wall. Ideally, install a false back in the wall unit and line the space between the back of the unit and the wall with batts of acoustic insulaton.

To play loud music or practice an instrument without disturbing anyone, line the walls of your room with additional drywall to increase the mass (see page 88). Consider installing a double door, as is done in music practice rooms.

In all aspects of noise reduction, the smallest air path can render soundproofing efforts worthless. Tight air seals using cork or rubber gaskets are effective, but remember to make sure such rooms are well ventilated. Many of the solutions to airborne noise are similar to those for sealing warmth into buildings. They can have a combined benefit (providing ventilation is addressed) since both heat and sound are transmitted, in part, through air paths.

PLANTS

THE FLOWERS, LEAVES, AND SUPPLE forms of plants have long inspired decorators, painters, carpet weavers, and architects. But the importance of plants for humans goes beyond aesthetic enjoyment—plants transform the sun's energy into life. Only an urbanized society—one disassociated from the landscape—would ever need to remind itself of the importance of plants by conducting experiments to show that our heartbeats slow when we look at vegetation. Plants in the home can create some of the magic of gardens and, in sufficient numbers, they can soften the acoustic qualities of a room. Even more important, plants can contribute to healthy indoor air quality.

Plants are always at work. Through photosynthesis, they convert sunlight into energy, give off oxygen, and absorb carbon dioxide. They also transpire through the leaves and roots and help to modify humidity in the surrounding air. The foliage, roots, and soil create a microclimate around the plant, which has a measurable effect on the space it occupies.

Pioneering research at NASA by Dr. B. Wolverton, supported by research in Sydney, Australia, has shown that plants can process and absorb many of the unhealthy substances found in homes that contribute to poor indoor air quality and can lead to illness. These include formaldehyde, VOCs (volatile organic chemicals), xylene, and ammonia. Plants also reduce airborne bacteria and fungi, and citrus plants appear able to sterilize air. Allowing the air to reach all parts of the plant, including its soil and microorganisms, contributes to this process. The larger the leaf area, the better, and plants with many smaller leaves can be just as effective as large-leaved plants.

HOME FOR PLANTS

An ideal living room, this large, light, plant-filled area is only partly enclosed with glass to balance solar gain with the loss of heat in winter.

A single plant provides a striking visual element in this classic setting *(left)* and also helps clean the air.

The research suggests that certain plants have an effect on particular chemicals found in the home. If you are unsure about the chemicals you need to deal with, there are some plants that are effective against a range of the more common household emissions. The spider plant, bamboo, rubber plant, peace lily, areca palm, and English ivy, for example, appear effective against formaldehyde, carbon monoxide, benzene, and xylene. Another study has shown that plants reduce the amount of particulates in indoor air—they seem to adhere to plant surfaces.

Plants also give off moisture into the air, increasing indoor humidity. In winter, air is naturally dry and is made even drier by most heating systems, causing a range of respiratory and allergic disorders. Plants can help to counteract this and bring humidity up to healthy levels of 40 to 60 percent. Too much humidity, however, allows the growth of molds and biological contaminants.

PLACING PLANTS

Although research on the beneficial effects of plants is relatively limited as yet, the evidence is sufficiently strong to make them an integral part of any safe home, rather than simply decorative items. It is suggested that one plant should be allowed for approximately 10 square yards of floor space, assuming average ceiling heights of 8 to 9 feet. This means that you need two or three plants to contribute to good air quality in the average domestic living room of about 20 to 25 square yards.

Although many plants like light, they do not all have to be placed near windows. Many indoor plants originated in the dense shade of tropical forests and have a high rate of photosynthesis. These are ideal for the home and can be placed in darker corners. When positioning plants, try to

Plants thrive in groups *(left)*. Here, they are placed next to a tree trunk used as an architectural feature.

FLOWERS

Cut flowers may not remove toxins and fumes, but they help make a room look fresh and bright.

strike a balance between light and ventilation because the effect of plants on indoor air pollution appears to be reduced if they are set in a draft. Think about the type of plant, the temperature, and the use pattern of a room. Sometimes trial and error is the only way to decide which plant will survive where. Place plants close to areas where you may spend long periods of time, such as desks and computer workstations, where they help to soak up harmful emissions.

Dr. Wolverton's research has shown the following plants to be the most effective all-around in counteracting offgassed chemicals and contributing to balanced internal humidity. Most are easy to maintain.

▶ Areca palm (*Chrysalidocarpus lutescens*)
▶ Reed palm (*Chamaedorea seifrizii*)
▶ Dwarf date palm (*Phoenix roebelenii*)
▶ Boston fern (*Nephrolepis exaltata* 'Bostoniensis')
▶ 'Janet Craig' dracaena (*Dracaena deremensis* 'Janet Craig')
▶ English ivy (*Hedera helix*)
▶ Australian sword fern (*Nephrolepis obliterata*)
▶ Peace lily (*Spathiphyllum wallisii*)
▶ Rubber plant (*Ficus elastica*)
▶ Weeping fig (*Ficus benjamina*)

AIR CLEANERS

Ficus plants *(above)* and the peace lily *(above right)* are both effective at removing toxins from indoor air.

HEALTHY AIR

Two or three plants such as Dracaena *(right)* are enough to ensure healthy air in a room.

SCENT

S MELL IS PERHAPS ONE OF THE MOST sensitive of our sensory tools, yet more often than not it is ignored when selecting materials and furnishings. But when something is seriously amiss in the home, our noses often give the first warning of possible danger—whether from a burning pan that could lead to a fire, a broken drain that could cause ill health, or escaping gas that might lead to an explosion. These warnings should not be ignored—our sense of smell is designed to tell us that we are breathing unsatisfactory air.

All too often, though, our noses are dulled through constant exposure to gasoline and other environmental fumes, stale indoor air, or offgassing from carpets, paint, and adhesives. We may think a smell has lessened over time, but we may simply have become accustomed to it, while the smell—and the potential health hazard—is still as strong as ever.

Harmful smells emanate from a range of substances within materials, either because the chemicals in their makeup are not stable or through abrasion and degradation from wear, water, light, and aging. Offgassing and biological contaminants—such as dampness and mold spores—are detectable only by smell, so your nose is your best sensing device for these problems. When selecting materials, think about their smell as well as their look and feel. Sniff a sample of synthetic carpet and then a piece of organic flooring and you will immediately notice the difference. Your personal safety is worth the few strange looks that you might attract when smelling a material or object in a shop.

SCENTING THE AIR

The scent from a huge display of spring flowers and blossom fills this room and sweetens the air. The flowers are perfectly positioned in front of the large window, where the warmth of the sun's rays helps to release their delicate fragrance.

REMOVING BAD SMELLS

If a material used in your home smells unpleasant, it may
be unsafe. If possible, remove the source of the smell and
introduce fresh air. If you cannot remove the item causing
the offending smell, you could install a filter device. Filters
contain either charcoal (activated carbon), which is good
for removing smells from solvents, fuels, and alcohol, as
well as body and cooking odors, or a mineral called
zeolite, which is most effective for ammonia and urine
smells from pets. Both types of filters work by a process
called adsorption—the gaseous molecules adhere to the
porous materials—but the filter materials become ineffec-
tive in damp conditions. Filters will not remove formaldehyde, sulfur, or nitrogen oxides so they should not be seen
as an alternative to removing very unhealthy substances.

A traditional—and gentler—way of eliminating odors
such as cigarette smoke is to burn candles. Apples also
absorb odors but are effective only in small spaces. Avoid
spray deodorizers—most of these do not remove the
offending smell, they simply mask it by injecting other
chemical substances into the air.

A FRAGRANT HOME

Conversely, we know how welcome certain smells can
be—sea air, scents of the open countryside, fragrant flowers. The contribution of these scents to a healthy home is
as important as that of silence or light. The sense of smell
is so integral to our health that a system of healing called
aromatherapy combines the beneficial powers of fragrant
essential oils with massage to improve health and well-
being. In the home, these essential oils can be used in
vaporizers to scent the air. A few drops of oil are added to
water in a small ceramic or earthenware container and
heated by a candle. As the oil warms, its scent wafts out
into the room. Try lavender in the bedroom to encourage
a good night's sleep, or sandalwood to create a relaxing

atmosphere in a living room. Oils can also be added to candles, polishes, and potpourri.

Other ways of making your home fragrant include placing vases of sweet-smelling flowers or bunches of aromatic herbs in every room. Herb sachets can be tucked into drawers and cupboards, and natural cedar blocks are an effective way of discouraging moths in clothing—we like the odor, but they don't.

Smell has undeniable power to activate the imagination and trigger memories and atmospheres. Everyone loves the aroma of freshly ground coffee and the smell of baking bread can take you back to your mother's kitchen. One of the many advantages of selecting natural materials for the home is that they smell good—rush and grass floors, wood such as cedar and pine, and natural vegetable-based oils and wax treatments on wood and other surfaces all have their own delightful, evocative fragrance.

Ways of keeping your home healthy and fragrant include the following:

▶ Remove any materials that smell of chemicals or give off strong vapors.

▶ Turn off any combustion appliance at the slightest hint of gas or odor, and have it checked.

▶ Arrange plenty of free air circulation if you have to work with strong chemicals.

▶ Ensure proper ventilation in all rooms, particularly bathrooms and kitchens, to avoid an odor build-up.

▶ Always ventilate enclosed spaces, such as cupboards under the stairs or cellars, particularly if they are prone to dampness.

▶ Don't use deodorizer sprays.

▶ Make your home fragrant with fresh flowers, herbs, and essential oils instead of chemicals.

CAUTION

Never ignore the smell of burning—or any odors that come from gas appliances. They can be fatal.

ELECTRICITY

THE USE OF ELECTRICITY, PERHAPS more than anything else, distinguishes homes today from those of the pre-industrial past. Electricity makes our lives infinitely easier, but it also poses problems for our planet and may even damage our personal health. Whether or not dangers exist is hotly debated at the highest scientific levels. All I can hope to do is to identify some of the issues that many people consider a health threat in the home, and suggest precautionary actions that may minimize any risks.

X-rays, microwaves, and other special and powerful electrical fields are universally accepted as dangerous. It is the weaker electrical fields encountered everywhere in daily life that cause continuing disagreement among scientists. Two factors make it difficult to form a definitive view. First, low-level electrical and electromagnetic fields are invisible; second, any effect on our bodies arises from a slow build-up over time. This build-up may not cause any apparent damage to most of us, but if it becomes sufficiently great or if your immune system is already weak, the effects may overcome the body's natural tolerance and spill over into noticeable symptoms.

With the proliferation of electrical equipment, including computer screens and mobile phones, our exposure to electric and electromagnetic fields, other than those that occur naturally, is increasing all the time. Illnesses linked to electrical stress range from headaches, low-level fatigue, disturbed sleep patterns, and inability to concentrate to chronic fatigue syndrome, epilepsy, multiple sclerosis, disturbances of the nervous system, and cardio-vascular problems. Some of these illnesses seem to have developed in the last 50 years and appear to be part of the significant growth in immune-deficiency diseases for which no one has yet conclusively proved a cause. It is significant that the advice from the U.S. government is to avoid risks until more is known about this subject. The relatively recent introduction of powerful, yet invisible, electromagnetic technologies into our lives means that we are, in effect, part of an experiment, the outcome of which we are unlikely to know for generations. Skeptics should remember that when X-rays were first discovered, no one gave any thought to their dangers, yet today their dangers are universally acknowledged.

ELECTRICITY AND OUR BODIES

Electricity is created by the vibration of energy, and it has long been known that molecules vibrate when they absorb or emit electromagnetic fields. Many of our body's processes, particularly those linked to neurological activity, operate through extremely low-frequency electrical charges. Since household electricity is so much more powerful, it seems likely that it could cause disturbances to the small but vital electrical charges in our bodies.

Electricity produces two fields of force that can affect us: electrical fields and electromagnetic fields. Their impact on us is determined by their strength and by the length of time we are exposed to them. Electricity, rather like water in a pipe, remains active in cables all the time, so even when we are not using light or power, electrical fields in buildings exist. Like ripples in a pond, electrical fields get weaker as the distance from the source increases, and they are absorbed by any materials that conduct electricity—metal objects, walls, even people. Therefore, protection from the effect of electrical fields is relatively easy to achieve by increasing our distance and creating physical separation from them. The Swedish government, which does recognize that there may be risks, advises keeping 3 feet away from any field-generating equipment. So, for example, try not to put your kitchen table next to the refrigerator or microwave, or your bed near a night-storage heater or a fuse box.

Electromagnetic fields are more problematic because, while their effects fall off with distance, few materials exist

A CAREFUL ARRANGEMENT
The table in this eat-in kitchen is placed so that
people are seated well away from any appliances
that may generate electromagnetic fields.

intense. Normally two or more power points supply electricity to appliances such as the lights, radio, electric clock, baby monitor, and telephone. In addition there may be a television nearby, with a remote control at the bedside. Electric blankets are the worst offenders of all because they effectively wrap the body with electrical fields. Electrical interference with patterns of sleep is thought to disrupt the essential restorative function of sleep, which seems to arise from electrical activity in the brain.

A device called a demand switch allows you to switch off the electric current in the bedroom at night. The switch can be fitted to individual circuits on the service panel. These supply a small but continuous, safe, direct current to the circuit, cutting off the electricity until you activate the switch an any appliance. Before fitting a demand switch, seek the advice of a specialist, as you will need electricity supplies at night to run your furnace, clocks, water heater, refrigerator, freezer, and communication equipment that operates automatically, such as a fax.

TVS, REMOTE CONTROLS, AND COMPUTERS

These appliances generate high levels of electromagnetic fields, but if we don't stay too close for too long, they should pose few problems. General advice is to stay at least 3 feet from the set when watching television. Avoid keeping a remote control close to you for long periods. Remote-control devices also waste energy. Because the set remains in the "on" or "standby" mode even when switched "off" by the remote, it uses almost as much electrical current as when fully functioning. Televisions may remain on "standby" for hours or even days, and the waste of energy is so great that the British government is considering legislation to prevent manufacturers from producing sets with remote capacity.

Electromagnetic fields emanating from computer screens are also a potential danger, although the increasing use of flat-screen technology, which operates without electromagnets, may soon remove this hazard. Sweden first introduced safety standards after studies on animals

that offer any protection. The fields pass through most building materials (except lead), people, and the ground. The problem is compounded because much of the equipment generating these fields is used in close quarters—computer screens, televisions, radios, microwaves, and mobile phones. The only way to avoid potential danger is to handle such equipment at a distance when possible and to minimize the length of time that you use it.

ELECTRICAL STRESS IN THE HOME

Electrical stress in rooms where you remain in one place for a long period, such as the bedroom, is likely to pose the greatest danger. Many bedrooms have a concentration of electrical appliances beside the bed, near the sleeper's head—just where the electrical activity in the body is most found evidence of the adverse effect of exposure to radiation from computers. Studies in the United Sates and Canada on pregnant women have given similar findings. The evidence is not yet conclusive, but it is sufficient to urge caution. Most radiation comes from the sides and rear of a screen so the proximity of anyone else in the room should be considered.

KITCHEN APPLIANCES

A normal electric oven or range has a significant electric field, which becomes negligible at a distance of about 3 feet. Other kitchen appliances, such as mixers and blenders have fields induced by their motors, but since these are used for such short periods they shouldn't be too harmful. Microwaves use powerful magnetrons, which produce strong magnetic fields. They cook food by agitating the molecules with very high frequencies. The reason why the cook is not cooked with the food is because, theoretically, the casing of the oven is constructed to contain the microwaves. But appliances seldom perform at 100 percent efficiency and they deteriorate with use. The fact that the appliance is acknowledged to be dangerous and we rely on a shielding mechanism is made even more worrying when we discover that scientists in different countries advise different levels of safety. A microwave considered safe in most countries is considered unsafe in Russia. Russian scientists—respected pioneers in health—believe that anyone using a non-Russian microwave oven may become ill. They specify radiation levels that are 1,000 times less than those specified in the United States. Such divergent views about safety standards should give cause for concern. Have your microwave oven checked regularly for electromagnetic leakage. And try to keep it as far away as possible from where people may sit.

PRECAUTIONARY MEASURES

There are many uncertainties on the issues raised by electrical and electromagnetic fields, and no one can establish the extent to which they will be susceptible. But anyone who has persistent symptoms of illness not attributable to any known cause, or who may be wondering about a lack of personal energy, might be wise to at least give these matters consideration.

It is possible to buy or rent detectors that can identify "hot spots" of electromagnetic activity in any internal environment. Electromagnetic fields are measured in milligauss. Since research on these is at such an early stage, there are no clear guidelines about safe strength of fields, and the question of what is practical is also relevant. A level of 2 milligauss appears to be a reasonably achievable maximum, below which it appears less likely to be risky. Use measuring devices to establish the strengths of fields. If you detect fields of 2 milligauss and above in areas where anyone spends much time, you might want to consider some of the following ideas to minimize risks.

► If you can, limit the time you spend in areas with electromagnetic fields.

► Since it is difficult to manage without electrical equipment, ensure that those you have comply with current safety standards.

► Have microwave ovens checked annually for electromagnetic radiation.

► Arrange furniture so that field-generating equipment is as far away as possible from positions where people spend any length of time. Don't forget about equipment on the other side of a wall.

► For mobile phones and other appliances that you do need to be close to, keep their use as brief as possible.

► Make sure that children do not sit or lie within 3 feet of a television screen.

► Do not leave televisions in the "standby" position.

► Do not seat anyone closely behind a computer screen where their electrical fields are strongest.

► Try to avoid placing beds along walls adjacent to, or on floors immediately above, the electric service panel.

► Headboards should be at least 3 feet from electrical outlets and equipment such as clock radios and alarm clocks.

► If you do use an electric blanket, unplug it rather than turn it off on the blanket's switch.

► To ensure your body is shielded from electrical stress when in bed, obtain a protective magnetic sheet to lay under the mattress. It is claimed that this will attract all surrounding electrical fields and ground them.

► Consider installing demand switches (see the opposite page) on bedroom circuits.

Chapter Three
MATERIALS

FLOORING

THE FLOOR IS PERHAPS THE SINGLE most important factor in establishing the feel and quality of a room. And from a practical point of view, it is the first surface you should choose. Flooring is subject to more stringent demands than any other surface and, since it is both difficult and costly to change, you need to make sure it will meet your practical and aesthetic requirements. Get your floor right and it will give you endless satisfaction; get it wrong and it could be a daily headache.

Floors also play a crucial role in creating healthy indoor air. Not only is the floor the largest dirt-collecting surface, but it can also be a source of dirt: The abrasive action of feet degrades the surface and adds to the amount of particulates in the air. These settle on the floor and are stirred up when you walk on the floor. A healthy floor is a clean floor—whatever it is made of. There is no doubt that a clean carpet will be healthier than a dirty hard floor, but the general view is that harder floors, provided they are kept clean, are safer. In global environmental terms, most flooring materials require considerable resources, so it is worth seeking out those made of recycled materials.

CHOOSING YOUR FLOOR

The range of floor coverings is so vast and making the right choice is so important that it may be useful to work through a list of factors to help you reach a decision.

1. Look at the nature and condition of the existing floor structure to establish the possible options:
▶ Will the structure support a heavy flooring material?
▶ Are there level problems that might limit the thickness of a floor covering?
▶ Does the covering need to prevent noise transfer through the structure to rooms below?
▶ Is the floor so uneven that a thin covering will wear at high spots?
2. Determine the demands that the floor must satisfy:
▶ Will the floor be exposed to water, grease, or excessive dirt?

▶ Is it an area that will get a lot of rough use?
▶ Will people walk barefoot on the floor?
▶ Will children play on it?
3. Consider the appearance and feel you want in the space and other needs the flooring might need to address:
▶ Is the acoustic quality of the flooring important?
▶ Do you want a floor that reflects light to make a brighter room?
▶ Do you want a floor that absorbs heat for solar gain?
(See pages 48 and 66 for the ways in which floors affect the temperature, light, and acoustic properties of a room.)

Once you have decided on some possible options that might suit your needs, assess your choices for their environmental performance and how they meet the criteria listed in Chapter One. The chart on page 122 summarizes the qualities of different materials from an environmental point of view. Since each material is different, it is important to take account of the qualifying notes as well as the particulars of your own installation.

The most successful floors are those that appear to be part of the structure of the building. In traditional buildings, flooring was generally made of a material appropriate to the surroundings—brick, ceramic tile, or flagstone in a country area; wood planks for homes near a wood. In an urban area, a stone related to the building material looks best. However fine a material may be, it may not look right if it is out of context with its surroundings.

STONE

Stone, including marble and slate, is one of the most beautiful and environmentally sound of all flooring materials. It has no adverse effect on internal air quality and satisfies most environmental criteria: It is readily available, requires little energy to produce, and gives off no polluting emissions in production. It is also immensely durable and can be recycled again and again. Even if discarded, it won't cause pollution. If possible, select a stone that is relatively local to avoid using energy in its transport.

WOOD FLOORING

A wood floor is warm and reflects
light. It also makes a perfect
background for colorful rugs.

The main environmental question to think about when considering stone flooring is whether the resource is being depleted or the landscape is being destroyed through the stone's quarrying. Generally, stone is unlikely to be exhausted, except in rare examples of special types, such as Portland or Purbeck stone. It is difficult to assess the effect that quarrying may have in faraway locations, so play it safe and purchase your stone locally. If that's not an option, search out a reputable seller and try to verify his sources for stone so you know they go easy on the environment.

In design terms, stone is extremely attractive and practical. It is often thought to be cold, but using a soft rug on top of stone will add warmth and comfort. Stone is also ideal for use with underfloor heating systems—its density allows it to both store heat well and radiate it efficiently (see page 66).

CERAMIC, BRICKS, AND TILES

For centuries, fired clay has been used all over the world to make floors, in forms ranging from simple sun-baked bricks to elaborate glazed tiles. One of the most attractive features of traditional ceramic tiles made of local clay is that they bring regional characteristics to interiors—think of tiled floors in French farmhouses or Italian palazzos.

Ceramic tiles rate very highly from an environmental point of view. Ceramic material (clay) exists in abundance and its processing is generally simple, relatively clean, and uses few chemicals. In large-scale commercial production, gas-fired kilns are often used, but in "native" production, wood fires are more common. Small quantities of heavy metals are used to color glazes, but the total level of pollution is relatively low compared to that associated with many other building materials. In terms of indoor air quality, ceramic material is stable and quite safe.

CLASSIC FLOORS

A combination of glazed and unglazed tiles combine into a simple pattern with a decorative border *(left)*. Stone slabs have such character that they are perfect on their own and need no other adornment *(above)*.

Clay is made waterproof by being fired at high temperatures—the higher the temperature, the denser and more waterproof the tiles. This process is called vitrification. Fully vitrified tiles are hard and completely waterproof. They are usually known as quarry tiles.

Traditional red terra-cotta is fired to a relatively low temperature and makes softer tiles. Although common in Mediterranean-style buildings, soft (unvitrified) tiles are less practical because they are not waterproof and are subject to frost damage. Soft tiles can be waterproofed by glazing with either transparent or colored glazes. Common examples are glazed bathroom tiles or decorative Spanish tiles.

Tiles are almost indestructible and and can be used time and time again—in fact, they may well command higher prices when worn, further ensuring their reuse. At the end of their life they can be either formed into mosaics of broken tiles, used as hardcore layers on building sites, or crushed to make safe sands.

MOSAIC, TERRAZZO, AND CONCRETE

Mosaic was traditionally made from small pieces of marble or glass (still known by the Latin term *tesserae*) set into a bedding on a solid floor. This art form reached its zenith in Ravenna between 400 and 600 AD, when glass artists used colored pieces of unsurpassed brilliance, including gold and silver. The technique of setting small objects into a bedding still lends itself to endless inventiveness and is an ideal way of recycling materials. Almost any objects flat enough to make a floor can be used, including coins, sea shells, bones, and mechanical components such as cogs. The health and environmental credentials of the finished floor depend on the material used for the pattern (see the information on different materials in this

Brick *(left),* slate *(above),* and terra-cotta *(below)* are all natural materials, yet each gives a different look to a room.

POLISHED CONCRETE

Raw polished concrete flooring is an ideal partner for the rich hardwood used on the stairs *(left)*.

OLD AND NEW MOSAICS

The traditional mosaic *(below)* is made of tiny *tesserae* tiles. The simple plain stone tiles *(bottom)* are combined with mosaic pebble stripes to make an unusual floor.

chapter) as well as the materials used for embedding the design materials.

Mosaic floors have many practical and environmental advantages: They are hard-wearing, absorb and radiate heat from the sun's rays, and offer good opportunities for using discarded and recycled materials. With all the opportunities it offers for imaginative and attractive designs, mosaic flooring deserves much more widespread use in today's homes than it currently enjoys.

A polished bare cement or concrete floor is simple and attractive. Its color can be enhanced by adding marble chips or dust to the wet floor, which is then ground to a smooth finish. This is known as terrazzo flooring. It can be continued up the walls to form an integral cove or baseboard, and it creates a hard-wearing, stain-resistant, waterproof surface—ideal in bathrooms and areas of heavy wear. From an environmental point of view, concrete and terrazzo score high. Although concrete is a high-energy product, these floorings maximize the use of the main structure and no additional finishes and coatings are needed. However, they can be used only where the structural floor itself is concrete. Mosaic, concrete, and terrazzo are all ideal for use with underfloor heating.

SOLID WOOD FLOORING

Solid wood is beautiful, practical, and has made the finest floors for centuries. It meets all the requirements for an environmentally sound surface—it is a renewable resource, requires low-energy input, and is safe and biodegradable. It is also one of the easiest materials to recycle. Woods used for floors can be grouped under three headings:
▶ Softwoods
▶ Sustainable hardwoods
▶ Protected tropical and temperate hardwoods

Softwoods come from coniferous trees such as pine, larch, European redwood (not the California sequoias), and spruce. These grow mainly in the northern hemisphere, from Canada right across northern Europe and Russia. Relatively fast growing—a crop can be harvested in approximately 20 years—they are used for most wooden construction, floors, and furniture as well for engineered wood.

Sustainable hardwoods grow mainly in North America, Europe, and Asia. They come from broadleaf forests that are managed to ensure a continuity of regeneration and supply of such wood as oak, ash, maple, and sycamore. It is not commonly known that some old-growth temperate forests in North America and Asia are also being destroyed.

Tropical hardwoods come from rain forests in South and Central America, Africa, and Asia. A few are managed for proper regeneration, but others come from unregulated harvesting and should never be used. Teak, iroko, mahogany, and aformosia are among the better known of the protected species. These trees are essential to the stability of the rain forest habitat. Harvesting them causes ecological collapse, resulting in the loss of unique flora and fauna, which causes soil erosion—leading to the eventual transformation of a once immensely rich forest system into desert. This, in turn, destroys indigenous communities, as well as a great source of natural plant chemicals—a gene bank that may disappear before its potential is discovered.

There are various accreditations for tropical hardwoods, but many of them are dubious and are used mainly as marketing aids. The only reliable accreditations are those recognized by the Forest Stewardship Council (FSC), which operates internationally.

Consider these essential points when laying a wood floor:
▶ Select only certified hardwoods or softwoods and preferably wood that is locally produced.
▶ Don't use wood in areas where it would require heavy protection against wear or water.
▶ Use only natural oil or wax finishes (see page 138).
▶ Use recycled flooring wherever possible.

COMPOSITE AND ENGINEERED FLOORING

A wide range of products known as "engineered wood" is made up in various ways to look like solid wood, and can be used as flooring. These include:
▶ Boards with a thin (⅛ to ¼ inch) solid wood face glued to a particleboard backing
▶ Boards with a very thin (less than ⅛ inch) veneer of wood glued to a particle board backing
▶ Particleboard printed with a photo of wood grain
▶ Plastic sheets that contain no wood, printed with a photo to emulate wood

Some of the above products come unfinished and can be finished on site. Others have a factory-applied finish, such

RECYCLED FLOORBOARDS

The interesting patina of age and wear adds to the effect of color, grain, and texture to make reused floorboards an attractive feature in any room *(left)*.

HERRINGBONE PATTERN

Short as well as full-length boards can be reused for flooring. This herringbone pattern *(right)* makes the best use of short lengths, but requires careful craftsmanship.

as a thick clear vinyl film, over the wood veneer. Only floors with a real wood veneer create the look, sound, and feel of real wood. Some of the best products are indistinguishable from wood, even on close scrutiny.

These boards can be as thin as ½ inch, for laying over existing floors, and are generally (but not always) cheaper than solid wood. Overlay flooring with a rubber backing made from recycled tires is also available. The resilient layer accommodates unevenness in the subfloor and also provides some acoustic insulation.

The environmental aspects of these wood floors are not straightforward and depend on all their different elements—veneer, backing material, glue, and finish.

▶ Veneer is not significantly different from solid wood, except that much less wood is used.

▶ Particle- and chipboard should be assessed in terms of the type of particles used (usually wood waste), and the glues and bonding resins.

▶ Finishing coats of clear vinyl have the same negative environmental characteristics as sheet vinyl (see page 122 for more information).

▶ For the environmental impact of liquid-applied finishes, see page 132.

BAMBOO

Although it is a grass, bamboo is as strong as many woods and almost as dense and hard-wearing indoors as oak. Like any grass, bamboo grows quickly—as much as 8 feet per year. This means that pieces of a usable size are generated

STAINED WOOD

Wood flooring can be stained a light color to create a durable, easy to care for floor that also reflects light *(right)*.

from crops every 5 or 6 years—roughly six times faster than wood. Other great advantages of bamboo are that it grows on marginal land, does not need fertilizers or pesticides, and that it regrows from cut shoots and does not have to be replanted.

For centuries, bamboo has been used in its natural form as strong, flexible sticks. Now that its excellent environmental characteristics have been recognized, bamboo is being used more and more as a versatile and attractive flooring material. Just as timber is engineered into a number of forms, bamboo can be engineered into narrow or wide boards or panels, exposing either the face, the end, or the edge grain. Thick boards can be tongue-and-grooved for use in the same way as wood in making a structural floor on joists or on battens laid over concrete. Thinner boards can be used as overlay flooring, also in the same way as wood (see page 115). From the point of view of internal air quality, bamboo has the same advantages as other smooth surfaces, provided that no unsafe coatings or adhesives are applied.

CORK

Cork comes from the bark of the cork oak and has been cultivated in Mediterranean countries for centuries. An entirely sustainable crop, it is harvested from live trees that regrow their bark to give a new crop approximately every 9 years. Cork is an excellent flooring material. Its combination of flexibility, high insulation value, and resistance to water is a product of its structure—fatty materials make each cell a watertight compartment. It is ideal for areas where a combination of warmth and some water resistance is needed, such as bathrooms or playrooms.

Cork is available in tiles made from small granules, larger flakes, or slices bonded together with adhesive resins. Tiles usually measure 1 foot square by ⅛-inch thick, but planks of 3 feet x 7 inches x ¼ inch are also available. The quality of cork tiles varies—their durability depends largely on the quality of the bonding adhesives used. It is difficult to verify this on purchase, however, and the safest course of action is to use a reputable manufacturer. Beware of discounts or bargain offers.

Cork is a little warmer and softer than linoleum, but less durable. As with so many other natural flooring materials,

BAMBOO

Fast-growing bamboo *(above)* has long been used to make furniture. Strips can be assembled into long planks for environmentally friendly flooring material.

SAFE FLOORING

Bamboo *(below)* and palm wood *(below left)* both make hard-wearing, attractive floors. They are easy to keep clean and give off no harmful chemicals.

cork's practicality and its effects on indoor air quality and health are affected largely by the finish. It degrades easily if not protected with a durable hard-wearing coat and discolors if the protection is penetrated by water. Cork flooring is available unfinished, as well as with a variety of factory-applied acrylic or polyurethane coatings or a clear vinyl surface sheet. All edges and joints should be sealed. Ideally, use tiles that are partly finished with a solvent-free coating, then apply additional coats of the same material after installation (for sealers, see page 138). Cork can be glued to either wood or concrete structural floors. Make sure that you use a safe adhesive.

CARPET

Wall-to-wall carpet, though not as fashionable in recent years, has many advantages. It can turn an "unfriendly" room into a warm and welcoming space. Soft and comfortable underfoot, it provides warmth as well as acoustic softness. No hard floor is as comfortable for children to play on or for walking on barefoot in winter, and a thick carpet and underlay will also deaden impact noise. In older houses with drafty ground floors, carpet stops drafts and increases warmth. It can also cover floors of a poor or uneven quality.

Carpet is also one of the easiest floorings to maintain, provided you have a good vacuum cleaner. Because of its natural oiliness, wool has some natural resistance to stains, which makes wool carpet ideal even in areas of heavy use. Avoid carpets treated for stain resistance (see page 118).

Good-quality carpet lasts for many years. The best combination for longevity is generally considered to be 80 percent wool and 20 percent nylon. Artificial fibers may be extremely hard wearing but are unsafe in production and also tend to "ugly out" before they wear out, losing their color or pattern. This is generally because artificial fibers are difficult to dye and hold color less well than natural ones.

Before choosing carpet, weigh all these benefits against a number of concerns about carpet:

▶ Carpet is generally considered to be one of the worst culprits in creating poor indoor air quality, harboring particulates as well as dust mites, which thrive in the warmth of carpet.

CORK FLOORING

Cork is a safe, versatile flooring material *(above)*. It is warm to walk on and also helps to soften the acoustics in a room.

RUSH FLOORING

Traditional rush flooring *(below)* is warm and has a wonderful textured look. It is ideal on old stone floors because it can tolerate dampness.

► Carpet made in an industrial setting, even natural wool carpet, is highly damaging to the environment because of the extensive use of dangerous and polluting chemicals during all stages of production. The yarns in synthetic carpet are made from petrochemicals, with all the accompanying disadvantages.

► Chemically treated natural and synthetic carpets are a major component of waste in landfills. They do not biodegrade, and they leach out polluting chemicals.

CARPET BACKINGS AND UNDERLAYS

Many carpets have backings that are treated with anti-aging chemicals and adhesives made of styrene butadiene rubber (SBR), which is carcinogenic and should be avoided. In some high-quality carpets, the backing is woven into the pile rather than glued, which is preferable but expensive. Underlays should ideally be made from untreated wool-felt matting or recycled rubber.

Some manufacturers recommend that their carpets be glued to the floor, but this is a very unsound practice. A large amount of adhesive is used and when the carpet eventually has to be ripped up and thrown away, the floor surface cannot be used again for a different finish without considerable work. Low-tack glues that are meant to avoid this problem are available, but they are only partly successful and they, too, are generally solvent-based. A better solution is to simply use carpet tack strips along the edges.

ENVIRONMENTALLY SAFE CARPET

It is possible to find carpet that has much less impact on the environment. So-called "organic" carpet, made from natural plant and animal yarns, is pesticide free and not bleached or chemically dyed. The natural oil of lanolin in wool acts as a water and stain repellent. Wool is also self-extinguishing, so it needs no fire-retardant chemical applications. The yarns are woven onto backings of chemical-free jute or hemp. Hemp is being used increas-

ingly in environmentally sound carpets because it is naturally resistant to mildew, fungal growth, and fading. Generally, nontoxic adhesives are used—often natural latex rubber.

Carpets from vegetable yarns such as jute, coir, and sisal are also available in a range of natural colors, free from any dyes. Although they are often sold as "natural," they are not chemical-free unless it is definitely stated to be the case. Natural fiber carpets that are not chemically treated score reasonably well with regard to renewability of resources, energy used, and their ability to biodegrade.

A new environmentally safe floor covering is made from paper twine, which is woven with linen into carpets and mats. Thinner than carpet, it has a texture like a very fine woven cane seat and is available in a wide range of natural-pigment earthy tones. A nonslip surface made of water-based synthetic latex is applied to the back. Safer, closed-loop production methods have increased opportunities for making environmentally sound synthetic carpet. Carpet made from recycled soft-drink bottles made of PET (polyethelyene terapthalate) that would otherwise occupy landfills is also coming into production.

UNDYED CARPET

This plain, undyed carpet *(above)* has an intriguing ribbed surface that catches the light.

PAPER TWINE

Paper twine matting *(below)* makes a soft, durable covering that can be used on damp surfaces.

CARPET AND INDOOR AIR QUALITY

The chemicals involved in carpet and carpet padding production can contribute to poor air quality. As with textiles, the manufacturing process involves a wide range of chemicals that remain as residues in the fibers. Backings and adhesives, with their potential offgassing, present further health hazards. The smell of new carpet is, in fact, the offgassing of VOCs, which can continue for up to 6 months after installation. Many cases of fatigue and eye or mucous membrane irritation in office environments have been attributed to new carpet.

When buying carpets, choose products certified as safe by the CRI (Carpet and Rug Institute Indoor Air Quality Testing) label in the United States. However, compliance with the statutory limits of these agencies does not necessarily mean products are totally problem free.

PRECAUTIONS WHEN INSTALLING NEW CARPET

▶ Ask the supplier/installer to unroll and air the carpet before delivery to your home.

▶ Open all windows and doors during and after installation, and if possible run a fan to dissipate fumes.

▶ Do not occupy the room for up to 72 hours after laying carpet—or while there is still the residual odor from the carpet and adhesives.

▶ Vacuum the carpet thoroughly before using the room.

▶ Don't let a baby sleep in a room with a carpet that is less than 6 months old.

AREA RUGS

The best way to enjoy a safe floor and the softness and warmth of carpet without actually laying carpet is to use area rugs. Easy to remove for thorough cleaning (areas under furniture collect the most dust), they can also be rolled away at times when lots of dirt is being brought into the home by pets or children with muddy shoes. Flat-weave rugs such as berbers have no pile, so they harbor less dust than those with thick pile. Rugs last longer if

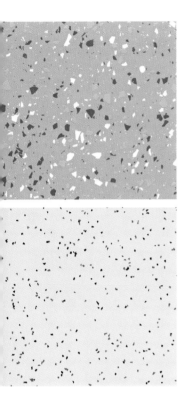

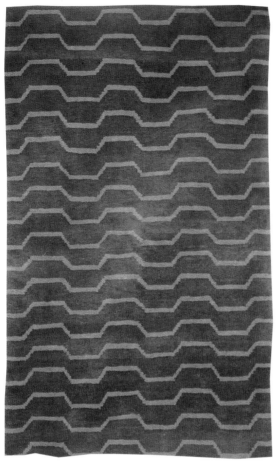

RECYCLED RUBBER

Rubber flooring, made mainly from recycled materials *(far left)*, comes in a variety of colors and patterns.

ETHICAL PRODUCTION

This modern, boldly patterned rug *(left)* was woven in Tibet using local wools and dyes. The makers certify that their rugs are produced by workers with acceptable labor conditions.

placed on top of padding or an underlay. And since the underlay is separate, it is also easy to clean.

A point to note is that rug weaving in many parts of the world involves child labor and poor working conditions. Whenever possible, buy ethically certified rugs.

RUBBER

Rubber sheet or tile flooring is durable, scuff resistant, and easy to maintain. It comes in a range of colors and textures, including round studs and a variety of raised grid patterns, which make it particularly useful in areas where a nonslip surface is needed. Rubber sheeting is also more resilient than other sheet materials and has better acoustic qualities.

Good-quality rubber flooring contains 75 percent natural rubber derived from trees and 25 percent synthetic (petrochemical) rubbers, fillers, and pigments. A material known as EPDM is the safest synthetic rubber, so look for that when purchasing. While the process of production does require high levels of energy, it is relatively low in emissions and waste. In the best-quality rubber flooring,

pigments are usually vegetable or mineral based. Offgassing is very low and the flooring can be recycled into lower-grade rubber products such as safety mats.

Rubber flooring can also be made from recycled car tires. These are ground, added to colored rubber granules, and reformed under heat and pressure into rubber sheets or tiles. Few pollutants are given off and the environmental benefits of putting discarded tires to good use are clear.

LINOLEUM

Once confined to dull colors, this warm, flexible, eminently practical material is now available in brighter shades, thanks to improvements in binder and pigment technology. Linoleum is made from entirely natural ingredients: Linum is the flax from which the base is woven, and "oleum" refers to the oils used—usually linseed and pine resins. Fillers of cork and ground-up wood waste are also safe and come from renewable sources. Production produces few polluting emissions and linoleum is also biodegradable. High temperatures are required during the "calendering" process, which makes the surface dense and smooth, but linoleum has far fewer environmental consequences than many sheet materials.

In use, linoleum is is an ideal material for the safe home—it is hard wearing, stain resistant, and easy to keep clean. It is suitable for areas that may be splashed with water, although it becomes slippery when very wet. It can be used wherever a flat, impervious sheet is needed and it is slightly softer and more resilient than sheet vinyl or tiles. Linoleum offers many attractive characteristics for use in all areas. Where a touch of softness is needed, use an area rug over linoleum. Just be sure to use a skid-resistant mat underneath the rugs.

VINYL (POLYVINYL CHLORIDE) FLOORING

In use, vinyl flooring is similar to linoleum, except that it is less resilient. However, vinyl is most unsatisfactory from an environmental point of view because it is derived from crude oil and requires large amounts of energy and chlorine to manufacture, although some chlorine-free PVCs are becoming available. PVC also contains dangerous chemicals such as phthalates, which vinyl manufacturers claim are "trapped" in the flooring and do not leach or escape during the use of the floor. While this may be true, the very use of such chemicals makes this synthetic flooring questionable when other excellent products are available.

In addition, vinyl flooring is virtually indestructible unless it is incinerated, and then it gives off dangerous toxic emissions. When it's left in a landfill, it leaches chlorine and heavy metals into the ground. Vinyl flooring is so problematic that a number of German municipalities have banned its use.

NEW RECYCLED FLOORING MATERIALS

In addition to recycled rubber, other flooring materials made from recycled products are coming onto the market. Recycled glass is used in combination with ceramic materials to make dense, stain-resistant floor and wall tiles. They are similar to glazed tiles but are fired at relatively low temperatures, and the process involves no toxic emissions. A United Nations program to discover sustainable products has also developed a floor tile made from ground mussel shells set in a cement compound, but these are not yet on the market.

FLOORING CHART

This chart summarizes in broad terms the environmental and practical aspects of different flooring materials.

✔ Good rating
◯ Medium rating
✗ Poor rating

FUNCTIONAL CRITERIA

	DURABILITY	STAIN RESISTANCE	DURABILITY IN WET A...
WOOL CARPET[3]	◯	◯	✗
ORGANIC CARPET	◯	◯	✗
SYNTHETIC CARPET[3]	◯	◯	◯
GRASSES/RUSHES[3]	✗	✗	✗
LINOLEUM[3]	✔	✔	✔
VINYL[3]	✔	✔	✔
CORK[3]	◯	◯	◯
RUBBER[3]	✔	✔	✔
SOFTWOOD	◯	◯	◯
EUROPEAN and U.S. HARDWOOD[8]	✔	✔	✔[4]
TROPICAL HARDWOOD[8]	✔	✔	✔
CERAMIC[3]	✔	✔	✔
MOSAIC[3]	✔	✔	✔
STONE	✔	✔	✔

ome synthetic carpet is recycled.

epends also on distance transported from source to user.

epends also on adhesives used.

ak is very durable but discolors when wet.

5. Can be dangerous on stairs if it becomes worn.

6. No material is slip resistant if covered with a film of water.

7. Available with rough surfaces to reduce slip.

8. Only sustainable timbers considered.

ENVIRONMENTAL CRITERIA

FTNESS	WARMTH	SLIP RESISTANCE[6]	SOUND ABSORBENCY	RESOURCE DEPLETION	ENERGY USED[2]	EMISSIONS DURING MANUFACTURE	EFFECT ON INDOOR AIR QUALITY[3]	CAPACITY FOR RECYCLING/ BIODEGRADING
✔	✔	✔[5]	✔	✔	✔	○	✗	○
✔	✔	✔	✔	✔	✔	✔	✗	✔
○		✔[5]	✔	✗[1]	✗	✗[1]	✗	✗[1]
○		✔[5]	✔	✔	✔	✔	✗	✔
○		✗	○	✔	○	✔	✔	✔
✗		✗[7]	✗	✗	✗	✗	✗	✗
○	○	○	✔	✔	✔	✔	✔	✔
○	○[7]	○	○	○	○	○	○	○
✔	○	○	○	✔	✔	✔	✔	✔
✔	○	○	○	○	✔	✔	✔	✔
○	○	○	○	✔	✔	✔	✔	✔
✗	✗	✗[7]	✗	✔	✔	✔	✔	✔
✗	✗	✗	✗	✔	✔	✔	✔	✔
✗	✗	✗	✗	○	✔	✔	✔	✔

WALL COVERINGS

WALLS ARE THE LARGEST SURFACE area in any space. Wall coverings, such as paneling, tile, wallpaper, or tapestries, allow us to modify the walls that we have to ensure that they are as environmentally sound and attractive as possible. The surfaces and texture of walls affect the feeling of a space in the following ways:

▶ Their ability to radiate cold or heat into or out of the room

▶ Their ability to absorb or reflect light

▶ Whether they create a hard or soft acoustic quality

▶ Their smell and effect on indoor air quality

▶ Their ability to "breathe"

Traditionally, the rough structural walls of dwellings were covered with linings to make them draftproof, warm, smooth, and easier to keep clean. But it is worth considering whether additional coverings on walls today are necessary. Working on the environmental principle that less is best, omitting wall coverings may be safest for both the planet and your personal health. This consideration, of course, needs to be weighed against the extent to which adding wall coverings might enhance the environmental performance of your house. The nature of the basic structure is crucial in this decision—if the walls are smooth and warm, any addition should be minimal. If, on the other hand, you can increase insulation, reduce drafts, or improve comfort, then a wall covering of one sort or another may have a great deal to offer.

RIGID PANELING

Wood has long been one of the most widely used wall coverings. Available locally, it is relatively lightweight, easy to apply, and offers an attractive surface for decorating. The insulating qualities of wood make paneled walls warm and pleasant to the touch. Traditional panels were made from whatever wood was readily available. The great houses of Europe employed the finest craftsmen to carve elaborate designs in oak paneling from their own estates, while modest cottages had panels of thin, rough boards taken from the nearby woodland. Both created warm rooms, in which the wood was decoration in itself.

Today, wall paneling is typically nailed to firring strips on the wall or to the wall framing itself, firred out where necessary to create a flat plane. Most paneling adds to the insulation of a room. You can improve the insulation further by lining the back of paneling with insulating material, but to avoid condensation problems, don't pack the space so tightly that there is no room for air movement. Environmentally safe insulation material includes shredded paper, flax, sheep's wool, cork, and coconut fiber. A reflective surface of aluminum foil facing into an air gap behind paneling helps improve thermal performance and avoids the danger of trapping condensation if ventilation is inadequate. Because aluminum foil is generally made from recycled aluminum, its production is safe.

Wall paneling offers the opportunity to solve visual problems such as uneven surfaces or protruding pipes. It can also be integrated with cabinets or doorways to create complete paneled walls. If you treat paneling as independent from the line of the existing walls, you can reshape rooms with curves and angled planes to create spaces where you can hide storage units and equipment such as televisions and stereos. This is a particularly useful approach in rooms that have several functions, such as a home office that doubles as a family room.

The void between the existing structural wall and the new inner lining, whether narrow or wide, forms a useful temperature buffer zone that moderates extremes of outside heat or cold. Avoiding condensation is essential, so you must maintain an air flow through any such space by leaving gaps at the top and bottom of walls and ensuring that any battens or internal shelves do not block the air flow.

WOODEN WALLS
Wooden boards line the walls of this room, providing warmth and an attractive textured surface.

Larger spaces should have airbricks or vents to bring air from the outside (see page 77).

Although wall paneling can be made economically from engineered wood, many of these are not environmentally sound (see page 113). Given that the paneling will probably be used over a large area, it's particularly important that they won't damage your indoor air quality. Softer fiberboards (check these to be sure they don't contain urea and formaldehyde glues) can be useful for softening the acoustics in a room and can add some degree of heat insulation to colder walls. However, they are not very durable as a wall surface.

The choice of wood, whether painted or veneered board, affects the atmosphere of a room. Darker woods like stained oak or the rich reds of cherry provide a warm, luxurious feel, while light oak, ash, maple, and pine give a brighter look. Wood can add an attractive scent—either from its natural resins or from natural wax polishes or oils. Paneling can also be made from bamboo—a durable material that meets many environmental criteria.

CORK AND LINOLEUM

Cork designed for use on walls tends to be softer than floor cork and has a more open texture. It is available in a wide range of colors and provides excellent thermal insulation, as well as softening the sound quality in a space. Cork is ideal in basements to soften and augment the hard finishes that may have been used on the walls. It is also good for children's bedrooms, where it softens the sound and provides a perfect surface for putting up pictures and posters. Light, natural corks can be stained with colored wood stains.

Linoleum is also available in a softer grade for walls and makes an attractive surface. Use linoleum on bathroom walls for a water-resistant surface without the hardness of ceramic tiles. As an added benefit, linoleum's flexibility allows you to bend it around corners to avoid unsightly joints.

CERAMIC TILES

Ceramic tile finishes on walls provide hard, impervious surfaces with harsh acoustics. They generally give a cold feel—welcome in hot climates, where tiled walls create

LINEN-FOLD PANELING
Oak paneling, intricately carved with a traditional linen-fold pattern, lines the cold stone walls of an historic home *(below)*. Other materials used in the room are also natural.

TILED WALLS
Glazed terra-cotta tiles make an attractive wallcovering that is hard-wearing, washable, and generally safe *(right)*. Their cool surface is ideal in warmer climates.

cool and restful interiors. Tiles for use on walls tend to be thinner than floor tiles and they can be larger, as they aren't subject to as much impact or weight. The advantages of tiles are that they are durable, waterproof, and available in a wide range of colors and patterns. (For information on the environmental aspects of ceramic material, see page 110.) Their effect on indoor air quality depends largely on the adhesives used to lay them.

PLASTERS

Since the earliest times, wall plasters of clay, lime, and gypsum have been used to block drafty cracks and create smooth surfaces. Clay, in particular, is the oldest as well as

SIMPLE PLASTER

Unpainted plaster can be an
attractive finish, and it needs very
little maintenance *(above)*.

A QUIET SPACE

This restful space gets richness and
texture from the grass coverings on
the walls and ceiling *(right)*.

perhaps the most environmentally sound of any material—it accounts for about 70 percent of earth. It can be dug virtually anywhere, it requires no energy to process, it's stable, and it biodegrades.

Forgotten for generations, clay plasters are coming back into use again. Designed to be left undecorated, they are available in a range of subtle earth colors, with textures varying from smooth to rough. Some clay plasters can be applied in layers as thin as ⅛ inch on masonry. If you're applying clay to plasterboard, use an adhesive priming coat to ensure that it sticks (see page 128).

Provided that clay plaster is applied to a thick (1-inch) backing coat, it helps to create excellent indoor air quality—it is vapor permeable and absorbs excessive humidity, which helps to prevent dampness. Clay plasters are particularly appropriate for use when renovating old, damp stone or brick buildings.

An interesting new development is plaster made from hemp and mixed with natural lime and water. It can be applied by trowel or poured into molds to make flowing forms, similar to a lightweight concrete. Furthermore, the hemp gives it a slight resilience somewhat like that of cork,

with all the advantages of warmth and acoustic softness. One of the most important environmental benefits of using clay or hemp plasters is that because they have an attractive natural color you can reduce the use of resources by eliminating painting entirely. If you do want to colorwash clay plasters, they combine extremely well with lime-based paints (see page 136) to make a "breathing" wall.

PAPER, FABRIC, AND VINYL WALL COVERINGS

Paper wall coverings date from 15th-century Europe, when single sheets of paper were glued to the walls to form decorative patterns and designs. Walls were also papered for health reasons—coverings were called "sanitary papers" because their oil-based inks made it possible for walls to be washed. Wallpapers were used extensively until about the middle of the 20th century, with craftsmen, printers, and artists of international standing, such as William Morris and Owen Jones, providing designs for mass-produced papers. Today, the use of wallpapers and similar coverings is questionable, since they use resources and require processing but have no environmental benefit. With the wide range of safe and durable plasters and paints available to meet most demands, it is more sound to eliminate the wallpaper and apply any decorative color or pattern directly to the wall.

Wallpapers are made of three principal elements, each of which may have environmental consequences: the face material—anything ranging from printed papers to grasses and silks; the backing material, usually paper; and the adhesive. Dyes and inks used in the face material are environmentally dangerous, as are the mold inhibitors included in the paper to prevent microbial growth in the event of dampness.

Wallpaper manufacturers have developed a standard for papers that establishes their environmental safety; this is stamped onto the paper. The standard ensures that monomer vinyl chlorides, formaldehyde, lead, cadmium, CFCs, and volatile plasticizers aren't used. Safer papers are becoming available that are made with as much as 60 percent recycled materials. The Forest Stewardship Council (FSC) also certifies some papers that use renewable wood sources. Fabric wall coverings should be subject to the same standards applied to fabric production for other household uses (see page 144).

Because of their durability and economy, vinyl wall coverings are gaining in popularity. Vinyl is derived from petrochemicals, and its processing includes dangerous plasticizers, chlorines, and synthetic inks and dyes. Vinyl

WALL COVERING CHART
This chart summarizes the environmental and practical aspects of different wall covering materials.

✔ Good rating
○ Medium rating
✘ Poor rating

1. Depends also on distance transported from source to
2. May be affected by amount of recycled material includ
3. Will be affected by material used for backing.

	FUNCTIONAL CRITERIA				ENVIRONMENTAL CRITERIA	
	THERMAL INSULATION	SOUND ABSORBENCY[3]	DURABILITY WHEN WET	DURABILITY WHEN ABRADED	RESOURCE DEPLETION[2]	ENERGY USED[1]
PAPER[3]	✘	✘	✘	✘	✘	✘
FABRIC & GRASS WALLPAPERS[3]	✘	✘	✘	✘	○	✘
THICK WEAVES/ TAPESTRIES FELT	○	✔	✘	✘	○	✔
VINYL	✘	✘	○	✔	✘	✘
THICK GRASS/ BAMBOOS	○	✔	○	○	✔	✔
SOFTWOOD	✔	○	○	○	✔	✔
EUROPEAN & US HARDWOOD[6]	✔	○	✔	✔	○	✔
TROPICAL HARDWOOD[6]	✔	○	✔	✔	○	✔
CERAMIC	✘	✘	✔	✔	✔	✔
SHEET METAL	✘	✘	✔	✔	○	✘

wall coverings are impermeable so, in addition to a risk of offgassing, they also add to poor indoor air quality by contributing to condensation build-up. Although a number of companies are moving away from petrochemical plastic coverings and using less-damaging materials such as wood and polyester fibers, it is best to avoid these products.

Woven-glass wall covering shares many of the practicalities of vinyl, but is made from natural, abundant, safe materials—quartz, sand, and stone compounds. This material has the advantage of being vapor permeable, while being thick enough to cover the imperfections of poor wall surfaces. Woven to give a variety of attractive textures rather like those of fabric, it is designed to be painted.

ends on chemicals used.
ends on adhesives used.
sustainable timbers considered

SIONS DURING FACTURE	EFFECT ON INDOOR AIR [5]	CAPACITY FOR RECYCLING/ BIODEGRADING [5]
✘	○	○[4]
	○	○[4]
	✘	○[4]
	✘	✘
	○	✔
	✔	✔
	✔	✔
	✔	✔
	✔	✔
	✔	○

WALL HANGINGS AND TAPESTRIES

Fabric wall coverings were one of the most important decorative items in homes in the past, and they played a significant part in keeping interiors warm. Fabric wall hangings brought color, pattern, and richness to bare rooms. Abstract patterns of flat kelim weaves hung in Bedouin tents; enormous allegorical tapestries adorned medieval castles. On stone walls and over doorways or windows, tapestries not only prevented cold radiation and offered warmth but also made space glow with color. Today they offer all the same advantages, and the growth of the craft of high-quality weaving creates wall hangings just as beautiful as any other artwork.

While the same question arises about the environmental soundness of using yet another layer to decorate wall surfaces, wall hangings offer the opportunity to enhance thermal as well as acoustic properties. The environmental aspects of fabrics are discussed on page 146.

WALL HANGINGS

Tapestries and rugs hung on walls look attractive, and they add insulation which helps to absorb sound.

BRUSH-ON FINISHES

BRUSH-ON COATINGS, SUCH AS PAINTS, varnishes, and stains, cover almost every surface in our homes. Their visual effects are obvious, but they also have an invisible but dramatic impact on indoor air quality. On a global level, manufacturing and disposing of paints is a major cause of environmental pollution. This section concentrates on these aspects of brush-on finishes and gives suggestions for how you can minimize their adverse effects.

TRADITIONAL COLORINGS

The whitewashed houses of Greece, the ochre-colored walls of homes in southern France, and the brown earth tones of African houses sit so comfortably in their respective environments because their colorings come from the surrounding landscape. The materials used to make these traditional colorings included mainly ground minerals, soils, and the less colorfast pigments of crushed plants. They were produced in small quantities and this, together with the particles of pigments, results in colors that vary in intensity and tone, making them much more attractive than the uniform look of modern paints.

The use of found materials meant that old-world paints had to be laboriously made up each time they were used, and their application was a labor-intensive and sometimes skilled task. Modern paints are formulated to avoid these disadvantages—they require no preparation and are quick drying, consistent in color, economical, and long lasting. But they lack richness, depth, and individuality—and the advantages they do have come at significant costs to our environment and personal health.

The structure of all paints is essentially the same. They have three main ingredients: pigments that provide color, binding agents to make the paint adhere to the surface, and solvents, the carrying medium for these ingredients and allow smooth application. Of course, paints also can contain a variety of additives such as fillers, opacifiers, fungicides, mold inhibitors, and softeners. These additives are meant to be beneficial to us, yet they, too, can cause problems.

MODERN SYNTHETIC PAINT PRODUCTION

The ingredients of modern synthetic paints—regardless of whether they are solvent- or water-based—are made mainly from oil-based chemicals and were developed after the discovery of aniline petrochemical derivative pigments in 1856. Thousands of chemicals are used in paint manufacturing (although not all of them are in one can!). Their processing uses huge amounts of fossil fuel energy and generates large quantities of waste, most of which consists of toxic emissions to air and water.

Organic solvents from paint manufacturing account for approximately 20 percent of the hydrocarbons that pollute the earth's atmosphere, and the production of one ton of solvent-based paint can produce as much as 30 tons of dangerous, mainly toxic, non-biodegradable waste. In addition, when paint or painted surfaces are disposed of, they leach chemicals and pollute air, earth, and water.

The chemicals in paint also affect air quality in our homes by offgassing slowly during natural aging, long after the initial curing period. While paint is generally considered adequately cured for practicable hardness within 48 to 72 hours, research shows that all paints offgas for as long as 6 months, and water-based paints can do so for up to 12 months. The World Health Organization (WHO) reports that painters suffer 20 percent more cancers than average, and 40 percent more lung cancer. PFO (perfluorocatanyl sulphate) chemicals, which have long been used in paints, have recently been recognized as serious carcinogens (see page 180).

Synthetic pigments used in paint contain a wide range of substances, including unsafe quantities of heavy metals such as cadmium, titanium, and cobalt, which can offgas.

WHITEWASH
Traditional whitewashing has a luminous quality that makes the wall as attractive as any decoration.

VISUAL INTEREST
In this modern home, whitewash containing a strong yellow ochre pigment *(right)* adds visual interest to the plain walls.

ORGANIC PAINTS
Organic paints *(above)* are safe to use and safe to live with. They also provide fresh, lively, natural colors.

Solvents and binders contain substances such as synthetic turpentine and volatile organic compounds (VOCs), known to be one the most unhealthy groups of chemical ingredients, which give rise to a variety of health problems (see page 180). Generally, the more durable the paint, the higher the solvent content. The oil-based paints normally used on woodwork, in kitchens, and in other areas of high wear have the highest solvent content. Each can of conventional synthetic oil-based paint can consist of as much as 70 percent of these solvents. Matte-finish water-based (latex) paints for walls may contain as little as 2 percent of solvents, but they do contain other dangerous chemicals such as toxic monomers.

The paint industry in both the United States and Europe is beginning to phase out high-VOC paints. Some paints are now classified according to their VOC content, which is identified on the label as follows:

▶ Minimal: 0–2.9 percent
▶ Low: 3–7.99 percent
▶ Medium: 8–24.99 percent
▶ High: 25–50 percent
▶ Very high: over 50 percent

As people have become aware of the dangers of some ingredients in paints—especially VOCs, which are easily smelled—paint manufacturers have been obliged to clean up their manufacturing processing and reduce the amount of solvents used. However, a useful measure of the dangers involved in paint is the EPA's list of polluting industries—paint factories are still among the heaviest environmental polluters in the United States.

WATER-BASED PAINTS

In developing water-based paints, manufacturers have merely substituted one set of dangerous chemicals for another, including acrylics. In fact, these paints contain more chemicals than the solvent-based types. The solvent replacements are harmful substances such as vinyls, acrylics, and acetates. Many dangerous emulsifiers, plus defoaming, neutralizing, and setting agents, are needed when solvents are reduced. In addition, water-based paints are subject to microbial growth, so preservatives and fungicides, such as formaldehyde and chlorinated hydrocarbons, are used. And most glossy water-based paints still typically contain 20 percent solvents. A review of safety in paints demonstrated that while water-based paints may be low in VOCs, they cannot be considered any healthier than solvent-based paints. During production, water-based paints also give off damaging environmental emissions, particularly carbon dioxide. Titanium dioxide is a widely used ingredient, the processing of which produces sulphuric acid emissions, although recently these have become tightly controlled.

A study published in 1999 by Green Seal, a nonprofit U.S. agency, examined 2,200 makes and types of paints and rejected 1,435 because they contained dangerous ingredients. The remaining 565 were tested for VOCs and other chemicals; of these, only 71 could be recommended as safe to use. This amounts to only 13 percent of the paints available. For a list of the safest paints, visit the Green Seal Web site (See "Sources" on page 182). The list of chemicals on page 180 indicates some of the most common ingredients in paint.

NATURAL ORGANIC PAINTS

No paint is 100 percent safe. But those that are made entirely from natural ingredients meet more of the criteria for products that are safe for the environment and for the home. The vegetable and mineral ingredients used in natural paints generally come from renewable sources and most, but not all, exist in abundance. These paints cause very few toxic emissions, have negligible effects on health, and biodegrade safely in land or water.

The traditional disadvantages of natural paints—for example, small batch mixing, variable supplies, uneven coatings, slow drying, and lack of durability—have been eliminated in modern natural paints. Processes for making these paints can follow the closed-loop, bioengineering principles that are just beginning to offer safer products in other types of manufacturing. Pigments and fillers are made from colored vegetable and mineral extracts. Binders and dispersion elements that replace VOCs are drawn from the natural oils from linseed, safflower, wood, tung, eucalyptus, hemp, and orange peel. A common resin is damarra, which comes from the meranti tree; other resins are extracted from larch, pine, mastic, and copal trees; and waxes come from the carnauba plant and beehives.

In all of these organic finishes, there are fewer ingredients than in synthetic paints. But they are not totally free of harmful substances. Solvents are still needed, but they are usually derived from vegetable extracts such as orange peel. Cobalt, cadmium, and titanium oxides are still used because substitutes of equal quality have not yet been found. But the most rigorous manufacturers strive to use the least harmful formulation of a substance—for example, one manufacturer uses titanium sulfide rather than the more harmful titanium oxide. Offgassing of natural solvents can produce irritants, but only during painting and until the paint has cured.

DECORATIVE PERFORMANCE

One of the most significant claims for organic paints is that they have a different visual quality compared to synthetic paints. Natural color pigments have a softness that is much more pleasing than the "hard" quality of synthetic paints. The different size of the particles in the paint catch the light differently, and their subtle inconsistencies give the surface life and variety. Most organic paints also offer greater vapor permeability than synthetic paints. This means they're better able to prevent walls from sweating or suffering from condensation, which can lead to mold and bacterial growth. Synthetic paints do not "breathe" as well, although some microporous paints are available for outdoor use.

In terms of performance, there is no evidence that organic coatings are inferior to solvent-based paints. Tests have shown that they tend to be marginally more difficult to apply, but they have greater color stability. Because no building materials are stable, paints need to be flexible; otherwise, they crack as the building settles. The acrylic in petrochemical paints causes them to become brittle while the natural oils in organic paints perform much better. The only significant disadvantage of organic, vegetable-based paints appears to be that they dry more slowly. But this seems a small price to pay for the advantages they offer.

WHITEWASH AND MILK PAINT

Whitewashes and milk (also called caseine) paints were commonly used to decorate houses before the introduction of chemical paints. Their subtle, flat colors have come to be so valued that many synthetic paint manufacturers produce paints that aim to match their qualities. Both whitewash and milk paints are made from simple ingredients. Whitewash is made from lime, which comes from burnt limestone. Although its production demands a great deal of energy, it is an abundant natural resource and requires no other chemicals. Caseine is a milk extract that has been an ingredient of paints and glues for centuries. It is mixed with chalk, linseed oil, and sometimes egg to make milk paints.

Whitewash is probably the most popular of these paints today. Traditionally, whitewash required the laborious and messy hydrating of quicklime to form lime putty, which then needed to stand for a few days before it could be used. Today, you can buy hydrated lime powder and mix it with powdered pigments to give a range of colors unrivaled by any synthetic paint. It is not, however, as long-lasting as lime putty paints. The impracticalities of whitewashing have been exaggerated—it requires no greater skill than painting, although a number of coats are needed. Note that whitewash is not suitable for application over existing paints, but milk paints adhere to almost any surface.

Whitewash and milk paints generally come in powder form for mixing with water; sometimes the pigments are added separately. Follow the instructions carefully—failure to do so might result in the paints becoming powdery on the wall. You can avoid this problem by adding more binders such as linseed oil. Take care when mixing whitewash—while lime is safe when carbonated (that is, cured by air), it is caustic on the skin. Always wear a dust mask and gloves when mixing any powdered substances.

CHOOSING SAFE PAINTS

If possible, select paints that have the largest number of natural ingredients or those with the lowest VOC content. Be aware that the best-quality, safest paint will require careful and patient application—all paints that claim to be "quick drying" or "one coat" achieve this convenience with the help of chemical ingredients. Also avoid, if at all possible, paints that contain chlorine or formaldehyde.

In terms of ethical issues, the natural paint manufacturers appear to score highest. The dangers to workers and devastating pollution associated with some of the large paint manufacturers are among the worst recorded—

Natural paints don't have to be a neutral color. Here *(left* and *far left)*, rich, glowing pigments add drama and character to rooms.

evidence of the scant attention they give to ethical issues. By contrast, some of the organic paint manufacturers are paying close attention to environmental issues, attempting to ensure that extracting resins in tropical countries is done in a way that will safeguard the stock of plant resources and create sustainable economies. To minimize transportation energy, they try to source vegetable ingredients cultivated close to the factory.

There are so many thousands of paint recipes that it is impossible to grade every one. The following list grades paints by general types, from the least to the most dangerous—whitewash and milk paints are the safest paints of all. The chemicals in paint (listed more fully on page 180) that cause most damage to the environment are generally also those that have the most adverse effect on indoor air quality.

1. Whitewash and milk paints
2. Vegetable and mineral paints—water-dispersion types
3. Vegetable and mineral—solvent-dispersion types
4. Synthetic water-based—low-VOC content
5. Synthetic solvent-based—high-VOC content

SAFETY PRECAUTIONS WHEN USING PAINT

▶ Avoid using paint where possible. Use natural oils or waxes on wood.

▶ Select the safest paint you can find.

▶ For environmental safety as well as appearance, apply paint sparingly.

▶ Reduce the amount of paint used by painting dark colors over light ones.

▶ Buy only the amount of paint you need to avoid waste, storage problems, and disposal issues.

▶ If using any high-VOC paints or two-part polyurethane coatings, wear the type of mask recommended by the manufacturer.

▶ Always wear a mask when spray painting, which is particularly dangerous since paint can easily be breathed in. Use a respirator mask—a dust mask is of little value.

▶ When painting or using strippers, keep doors and windows open. If working with solvent-based paints, use an electric fan to help disperse the fumes.

▶ Avoid paint strippers that contain dichloromethane, known to be a potent carcinogen. Use a hot-air stripper or scraper instead.

▶ Never throw away leftover paint. Seal cans tightly to prevent leakage and, if possible, take them to a paint-recycling center. For instance, some communities have recycling networks that arrange to recycle and reuse half-used cans of paint, making them available to low-income people or nonprofit organizations. Otherwise, take leftover paint to an approved chemical waste site, which your local municipality should be able to recommend.

STRIPPING PAINT

The desire for convenience and speed has driven manufacturers to develop ever fiercer and more aggressive solutions to make removing paint easier and quicker. The solvent DCM (dichloromethane), which is a severe skin irritant, and methylene chloride are prevalent in many paint strippers. Both ingredients are carcinogenic.

Water-based, solvent-free strippers are available from companies that manufacture natural paints. They give off no fumes and are significantly safer to use. The safest way to strip paint, however, is with either a hot-air stripper or abrasives and scrapers. Even poultice-type strippers use fewer chemicals than liquid strippers.

CLEANING BRUSHES

Brushes used with water-based paints can be washed, but rinse them in running water only after most of the paint has been washed away. For brushes used with oil-based paints, select a citrus-solvent brush cleaner. To minimize use of cleaners and water:

▶ Wipe as much paint as possible off brushes before cleaning.
▶ Do most of the washing in a container of water, thoroughly squeezing out paint from the bristles.
▶ When using a brush cleaner, use the same container for all colors by washing light colors first.

CLEAR WOOD TREATMENTS

Some clear synthetic coatings such as polyurethane varnishes—particularly the two-part systems that require mixing on site—are among the most dangerous of any finishes. Although extremely hard wearing, they include dangerous chemicals such as isocyanates and amine. Transparent stains are particularly high in the solvents or water-dispersal agents discussed above, which enable the stain to penetrate the wood.

To protect wooden surfaces from dirt and abrasion, it is much better to impregnate them with oils and waxes than to paint them with synthetic coatings. The Scandinavians have long known that oils, particularly tung oil, are as good as any synthetic finish, and use of these Scandinavian formulations is growing. Other examples of such natural finishes include boiled linseed oil and oils mixed with sol-

SURFACE PROTECTION
Traditional oils and waxes give floor boards richness *(below)* while protecting the surface from wear.

TRANSLUCENT STAIN
A light stain on wall and floor boards *(right)* gives soft color but allows the grain to shine through.

vents such as natural turpentine or citrus extracts. Oils and waxes leave the texture and grain of the surface visible while protecting it. Color tints can also be added. Oils and waxes also breathe particularly well, without any loss in durability, which is essential because wood moves all the time in response to changes in humidity and temperature. Finishes that contain natural oils and resins harden on contact with the air. Nonhardening oils, such as raw linseed, leave an oily surface that can attract dirt. The most beautiful protective indoor treatment for wooden furniture is to saturate it with a natural oil such as linseed or tung oil and then apply a finish of natural wax. Nothing compares with the finish achieved on old furniture over generations of polishing, but the wax does need renewing and polishing from time to time. For floors or woodwork surfaces, an application of tung or similar oils is probably the most practical finish.

Organic and low-solvent color stains, formulated with natural ingredients and spirits, are becoming more common today. Stains for indoor use do not need to protect wood from external weathering and can, therefore, be made with few harmful ingredients. Avoid using external stains and preservatives indoors because they have fungicide and anti-microbial ingredients that can lead to poor air quality.

GLASS

GLASS BEAMS

New technology allows beams made of glass to give maximum transparency while being strong enough to support the ceiling.

THE DESIGN OF LARGE WINDOWS FOR LIGHT, so characteristic of modern architecture, went hand in hand with the public health movement that followed the growth of the dark, smoke-filled towns of the Industrial Revolution. The importance of creating light-filled interiors continues to grow as we spend more and more time indoors.

Glass can help to create magical interiors not only by admitting light and sun but also by linking interiors to the outside world. But glass can also cause problems such as heat loss, overheating through solar gain, and poor soundproofing. These disadvantages can be eliminated by the careful selection of new sophisticated types of glass that improve insulation and soundproofing. New types of glass are so strong that manufacturers are now developing glass beams and columns that exploit the structural strength of the material.

Glass can help to create magical interiors by admitting light and sun

GLASS PRODUCTION

Glass fulfills many of the criteria for environmentally sound products. However, high-quality glass is produced in a few large factories worldwide so is not made of local materials. Glass is made of silica sand and mineral compounds that exist in relative abundance. The main environmental problem associated with glass is the amount of heat needed in its production, which involves large quantities of fossil fuel and consequent polluting emissions. Glass has no adverse affects on indoor health (apart from the risk of breakage). It is also safe when disposed of, although very small quantities of chemicals may leach out.

GLASS AND SOLAR GAIN

Unless windows are designed specifically for solar gain, it may be necessary to ensure that they don't cause your rooms to overheat when they are struck by the sun. A wide variety of anti-sun glass, made with coatings and metallic films designed to cut out solar gain, are available.

From an environmental point of view, however, maximizing heat gain in winter and using shading devices in summer is far better than using anti-sun glass. Solar gain is a useful and free source of warmth, but in order to make best use of it without becoming uncomfortable in the summer months, flexible shading devices are usually necessary. You can use shades, shutters, blinds, curtains, or draperies, all of which can be attractive decorative elements in their own right, to cope with changes in sun angle and brightness through the year.

THERMAL INSULATION

One of the main goals for an environmentally sound house is to minimize heat demand and the loss of heat through windows. The following products can help you achieve this goal, although not all to the same degree:
▶ Thermal-resisting glass, which is coated to prevent less heat from escaping through the glass (look for a "low-e" or "low-emissivity" rating)
▶ Double-paned units
▶ Double-paned units with argon gas between the panes
▶ Storm windows
The most effective way to increase insulation is to create air space between sheets of glass. Even more effective than air is when the space is filled with an inert gas such as argon. An air space increases insulation only if it is more than ¼ inch. A ½-inch or larger air space is ideal—but this is often difficult to achieve with existing windows; an additional storm window is a better idea. The most efficient form of window has the airspace between two sheets of high-performance glass is filled with argon. This is twice as effective as two sheets of ¼-inch clear glass with a ½-inch

air cavity, and four times as effective as a single sheet of ¼-inch glass. Triple glazing is common in northern climates where winters are icy, but it is not possible to install triple-glazed windows in existing window frames.

A number of special window and glass suppliers produce a range of tailor-made units that combine different types of glass, offering up to 60 percent more efficiency than straightforward double-paned units. But these figures need to be kept in perspective: Although the difference in window efficiency can be great, windows in the majority of homes amount to just a small proportion of wall area, so the dwelling's overall efficiency gain will be relatively small. Expensive new windows may, therefore, not offer the most cost-effective environmental improvement, and other ways of saving heat may be more cost effective (see page 62). Seek professional assistance or check with an advisory organization (see page 182) before embarking on expensive window changes.

Another factor that may affect insulation is the window frame. Since a frame can constitute 10 to 20 percent of the area of the window, it is important to ensure that it is made of an insulating material. Wood is an excellent insulator. Old metal-framed windows, on the other hand, are highly inefficient. Newer aluminium or steel windows may have what is called a thermal break, in which the cold outer parts are separated from the inner ones by an insulating core, so that cold is not conducted from the outside to the inside.

GLASS AND NOISE CONTROL

Changing the type of glass in a window can considerably reduce the amount of external noise that enters a house—providing that you take other measures, such as blocking air paths through window frames and fan openings. Sound-reducing glass is also available, ranging from specially treated single glass layers to sealed double-paned units. Double-paned units designed for thermal insulation will perform extremely well as insulators against noise; the greater the width of the cavity the better.

To obtain a good degree of sound reduction, however, it is almost certainly more cost-effective to add a separate secondary or inner window than to modify window frames to hold sealed double-paned units. By lining window jambs between the inner and outer windows with soft, absorbent material such as thick felt or fiberboard, you can achieve even greater noise reduction. (See the table and diagram on page 87 for more information on the degree of sound reduction achieved by different types of glass.)

GLASS AND SAFETY

Two factors determine how dangerous glass is when it breaks: its strength and resistance to breakage, and the sharpness of the pieces that result on breaking.

▶ Annealed glass is the type of glass most commonly found in homes. It's fairly easy to break, and when it does break, it shatters into large shards of glass. Single-paned annealed glass provides little insulation and doesn't block out noise very well.

▶Heat-strengthened glass is twice as strong as annealed glass, but it still has the potential to break. It is made stronger through a heating and slow-cooling process.

▶ Fully tempered glass is four times stronger than annealed glass. It is made from annealed glass that is heated and cooled quickly. When it breaks, it crumbles into many tiny pieces rather than dangerous large shards.

▶ Laminated glass is possibly the safest glass. It is made from two sheets of glass laminated on either side of a transparent film. It can be made from any type of glass. The laminating process gives the glass great impact strength, so when it does break, it will crack but remain intact, which makes it good for security purposes.

▶ Clear polycarbonate sheet (Plexiglas) is sometimes used as a safe glass substitute: it is virtually unbreakable but scratches easily and tends to have less clarity than plate glass. In addition, it's a plastic derived from unsound petrochemicals, so try to avoid using it.

Fire-resistant glasses are also available and in some types of dwellings, such as apartment buildings or houses with more than two floors, it is mandatory to use fire-resistant glass for any glass that separates kitchens from staircases and corridors. This is a specialist field, so if you're making any changes to existing glass or if you're using any glass in these locations, get advice from your local building inspector.

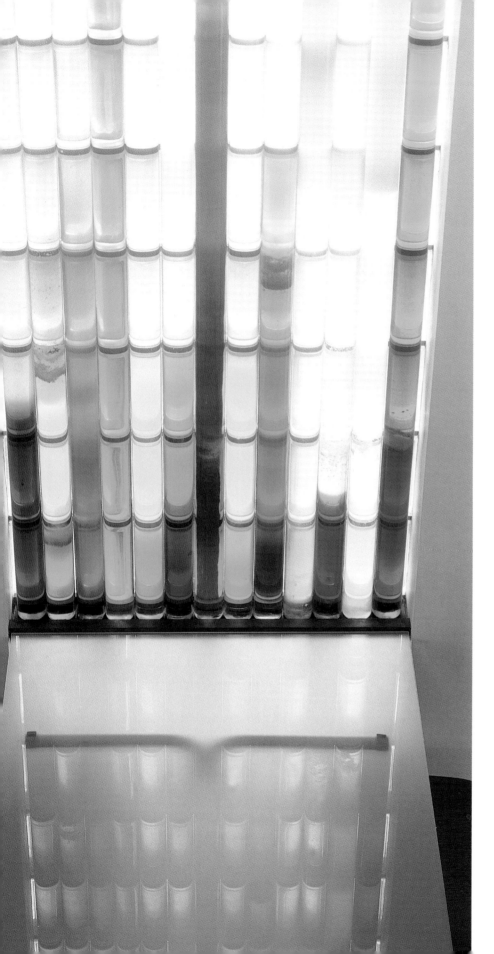

CHANGING LIGHT

Colored glass offers constantly changing effects as light conditions vary throughout the day—and year. It is also an ideal way of providing privacy while admitting light.

CAUTION

All glass in the home that is at risk of being broken—for example, glass that is lower than 30 inches above the floor, any glass in a door, or a glass panel within 1 foot of either side of a door must be certified safety glasses. Any clear sheets of glass that people might not see and could walk into should be marked at 4½ feet from the floor so that they are visible.

FABRICS

For style—add fabric; it can instantly transform a space and create a mood. For centuries, fabric was the primary furnishing element used to cover walls, windows, doorways, hard benches, beds, and tables in homes ranging from bare wooden huts to stone castles. The role of fabric in the home used to be so important that in the grandest houses it was the upholsterer who masterminded interior furnishings and employed the cabinetmaker and other craftsmen.

Fabrics help keep the home warm by providing insulation; they also absorb sound, creating a "soft" acoustic, and give physical comfort. Whether shiny, sparkling, crisp, supple, or soft, fabrics carry an array of stylistic messages—all conveyed simply by color, pattern, and texture. The gentle earth tones and rough textures of natural fabrics, for example, often suggest a safe, homey, comfortable look. But this bears no relation to the environmental or domestic safety of a fabric: That is determined by the extent to which chemicals are used in plant growing, cloth manufacturing, and fabric finishing.

TEXTILE PRODUCTION

Textiles are produced all over the world and are a major commodity in international trade. Their production is linked to the economies of third-world communities—and to those of the modern global chemical companies who sell these communities vast quantities of chemical fertilizers and pesticides. The chemicals are used to combat the diseases and pests that infest the plants used to make yarn fiber.

So many chemicals are used in the production of cotton, in particular, that it is a major contributor to global environmental degradation. While cotton is grown on just 3 percent of the world's cultivated land, it consumes 25 percent of worldwide production of chemical fertilizers and pesticides, which include DDT and pyrethroids. In adition, cotton is mechanically harvested, a process that often involves chemical defoliation.

Chemical-dependent agriculture has increased because insects have developed pesticide resistance, so more and more new products have to be used against them. And chemically fertilized land (as opposed to land fertilized organically) demands ever-increasing chemical use to sustain production. A vicious circle of destruction ensues, with increased spending on costly chemicals accompanied by a decline in production, which affects the economies of many third-world communities. Bioengineered crops create similar patterns of chemical dependency. The same issues are also associated with wool production, which can involve chemicals such as DDT and organophosphates. These have been banned for use on human food crops, but remain as residues on the fabric that we use in our homes.

PROCESSING FIBERS

The subsequent processing of both vegetable and animal fibers into fabric involves more chemicals, such as chlorine, formaldehyde, and polymer coatings, for desizing, scouring, cleaning, bleaching, preshrinking, and many other processes. Following this, the fabric is subject to further chemical treatments during mercerizing, dyeing, printing, softening or stiffening, and in treatments such as stain resistance, fireproofing, and easy care. Chemical residues left by the finishing and coloring processes can account for up to 20 percent of the weight of the fabric. You may feel comfortable with a fine cotton sheet next to your skin but, unless it was organically produced, what you probably have is a film of dangerous chemicals. In addition, these processes use vast quantities of water, which in turn becomes polluted with a variety of chemicals.

PURE LINEN

The texture and appearance of linen is so attractive, it does not need the addition of colorful dyes to enhance its beauty.

EMBROIDERED DECORATION
Traditional embroidery on natural cotton fabrics provides decoration while avoiding dyes.

Many of the processes described above arise from consumer demand for certain performance standards in fabrics. We, as consumers, can make a positive contribution to environmental, health, and ethical issues by instead demanding fabric that is produced from organically grown yarns, does not involve chemical processes, and is colored with vegetable-based dyes instead of synthetic chemicals. This would break the downward spiral of land degradation and the destruction of yarn-producing communities in the third world. It could also help us to create safe, attractive, and satisfying homes with traditional organic fabrics or with new fabrics made using closed-loop production processes, as described in Chapter One.

CHEMICALLY BASED SYNTHETIC FABRICS

Fabrics cannot be categorized simply as man-made or natural because many yarns and fabrics, such as rayon and acetate, contain blends of natural fibers, natural cellulose, and chemical-based filaments. Acrylic, nylon, polyester, and virtually all other synthetic yarns, however, are produced almost entirely from polymers derived from petrochemicals by unsound processes. They are generally less costly to produce than the natural fibers they attempt to emulate and offer supposedly beneficial performance characteristics, such as resistance to moisture, stains, shrinking, or crumpling. They may also be lightweight, quick drying, and easy to wash. But these synthetic fabrics all contribute to the serious environmental problems discussed in Chapter One.

Although it is true that some of the processes needed to transform natural fiber into yarn are not required for synthetic fabrics, it takes many other polluting processes to convert the base petrochemical materials into synthetic fibers. First, they need to be either dissolved in solvents or melted, both of which are high-energy, polluting processes. These yarns also need larger amounts of chemicals to color and wash them than natural fibers do.

The extent of the pollution caused by synthetic cloth manufacturing is demonstrated by the Environmental Protection Agency's (EPA) list of top polluting industries. Two of the three biggest polluters in the United States are manufacturers of synthetic yarns. Emissions include acetic acid, formaldehyde, solvents, chlorine substances, and other dangerous chemicals. Another disadvantage of synthetic fibers is that they can give off toxic fumes in fires. To prevent this, some fabrics are treated with a variety of chemical substances, including formaldehyde, bromines, and halogens.

SAFE, NATURAL FABRICS

As with other materials, the general environmental principle applies to fabric: The less it has been processed and the nearer it is to its natural state, the safer it will be. Some natural plant fibers, such as linen, flax, hemp, jute, and sisal (as well as some animal fibers), can be produced with considerably less processing and chemical treatment than cotton. The natural structure of these safe plant fibers consists mainly of cellulose, which makes them pliable, absorbent and strong. Each has its own characteristics, requiring certain methods of growing and processing, which have different environmental and health consequences.

Fibers such as hemp, jute, sisal, and ramie offer enormous potential to create a wonderfully rich range of furnishing options. They stand up well to wear, which helps them maintain their original appearance, and when they become waste they will harmlessly biodegrade. Organic fabrics are particularly useful in bedrooms—especially if you suffer from chemical or other allergic reactions.

Flax and linen are often confused, as they both come from the flax plant. Flax fabric is rougher than linen and is produced during the earlier phases of transforming the fiber into linen. Both are strong, supple, and absorbent, and have a natural luster that tends to become more attractive with age. Although flax is a limited crop because it requires fertile land and a maritime climate, it can be easily grown using natural crop protection methods such as soil rotation, rather than chemicals. Retting—the separation of the fibers from the woody plant—is achieved without chemicals by keeping the fibers damp over a period of time.

Hemp is extremely strong and has long been used for making products such as rope, burlap, and sailcloth. Because it is a bark fiber and not a seed fiber like cotton and flax, it grows well without herbicides, fungicides, or

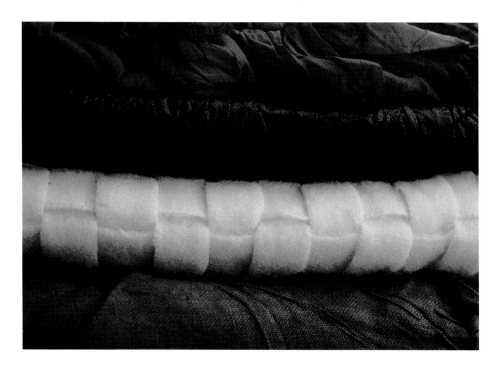

fertilizers. This makes it ideal for the production of non-chemically treated yarns and encourages the use of environmentally safe processes in the later stages. Although the yarn-producing hemp plant is not the same as its relative the marijuana plant, its cultivation is forbidden in the United States. Supplies generally come from China and, more recently, from eastern Europe.

Ramie is one of the oldest of all fibers and was used to make fabric in ancient China. It has a similar "natural" appearance to linen but is less costly to produce. Ramie takes dye easily and therefore needs a minimum of chemical additives for color-fast dyeing. It is absorbent like cotton, dries quickly, and is resistant to bacteria and molds, so it needs no special chemical treatments. It has a high luster but is rather rough, so it is often combined with other fabrics for softness. Its resistance to abrasion makes it a good fabric to use for upholstery.

Wool has many unique qualities that have been recognized since early times, and it is only recently that synthetic chemicals have been used in its processing. Wool makes beautiful fabric that needs little enhancing. It is naturally strong and resilient for its weight. Wool is also highly insulating, contains natural stain-resistant oils, such as lanolin, and is naturally fireproof. Untreated wool can absorb up to one-third of its own weight in water before feeling wet to the touch.

Organic cotton can be processed into fabric without chemical treatment. FoxFibre of California offers a wide range of fabrics made from organically grown cotton plants that have been bred to be self-colored and therefore require no dyes. Self-colored cottons have always existed, but their short fibers were suited only to hand production. Sally Fox of FoxFibre uses natural breeding processes to develop fiber lengths suitable for mechanized manufacturing, thus making these natural yarns a commercial proposition. They come in a range of natural earth tones—rust, cream, browns, and greens—and new colors are being developed. One of the great assets of these textiles is that the colors become more intense the more they are washed rather than fading as dyed fabrics do. The cost of undyed organic fabrics like these is still high—production quantities are so small they cannot compete with mass-produced cotton—but ounce-for-ounce, they use approximately 30 percent fewer resources to produce.

SAFE MAN-MADE FABRICS

New man-made fabrics are being developed for produc-

NEW CLEAN PROCESSES

Fabric made by the DesignTex company uses clean processes and safe chemicals *(above left)*.

NATURAL COLORS

This beautiful, safe multicolored Ikat fabric is made with natural, vegetable-based dyes *(above right)*.

tion by sustainable, clean methods, including the use of recycled materials. Lyeocell, usually known by its trade names Tencel and Cupro, is a wholly man-made fabric, said to be the only significant "new" fiber developed in many years. It is made entirely from natural wood pulp cellulose, without any toxic or polluting chemicals, and the majority of the processing agents are recyclable. It holds dye well, is absorbent and strong when wet, drapes well, and biodegrades easily.

Other new fabrics such as Climatex Lifecycle products set a high standard in clean production. This pioneering company has created DesignTex, a fabric made from worsted wool and ramie. The production exemplifies new safe processes.

Another type of environmentally positive fabric is made from recycled thermoplastic components. The United States alone discards 2.5 million soft-drink bottles made from PET (polyethelyene teraphthalate) every hour! This inert waste is ground up to form the base ingredient for fabric filaments—although dyeing these fibers may have the same impact as the dyeing of petrochemical fibers. The recycling process uses low energy because high temperatures aren't required; therefore, the release of emissions is low. Transporting waste is an environmental cost, but the waste problem is so great that any such attempt at using it

deserves to be supported. Recycled PET fabric is best known for fleece garments, but it is also used to make blankets and carpeting.

COLORING AND PRINTING

Adding color to fabric and creating patterns and prints are among our most rewarding decorative traditions. For centuries, naturally occurring vegetable, animal, and mineral dyes were used to color fabric, but today synthetic dyes are used, adding to the environmental damage caused by chemical-based fabric cultivation and processing. Dyeing and rinsing processes for coloring fabric alone generate over 17 gallons of waste water for every pound of fabric product. The average dyeing facility in the United States generates between 1 and 2 million gallons of wastewater per day!

Fabrics that are considered safe are either left as their natural color or are dyed using age-old recipes for naturally occurring dyes. This doesn't mean that the range of colors has to be limited, as demonstrated by the sumptuous fabrics made prior to the introduction of synthetic dyes in the 19th century. Those fabrics all used natural dyes—although admittedly some of the strongest colors contained heavy metals such as chrome, nickel, cadmium, and cobalt. Naturally dyed fabrics—which are quite the equal of any synthetic dyes—are still available today.

STAIN-RESISTANCE TREATMENTS

Fabrics are commonly treated with chemicals to increase their resistance to stains, but the safety of these treatments has recently come into question. One of the most common treatments, a worldwide market leader, has recently been withdrawn from some markets because it uses PFO (perfluorocatanyl sulphate), a chemical that enters human tissue and is understood to be carcinogenic. Research has shown that the only human blood found to be free of this product was in samples taken prior to the product's invention. The EPA is urging a worldwide ban on this common but deadly chemical. Mothproofing, too, uses contact insecticides that should be avoided, and fireproofing treatments involve a range of dangerous chemicals (see page 180).

CERTIFICATION OF FABRICS

Because the dangers of such extensive use of chemicals has been recognized, the certification of fabrics is more widespread than it is for many materials. A number of organizations in various countries offer labeling systems to certify that a fabric is safe. The criteria they assess are not entirely consistent, but they cover similar issues: environmental impact or ethical animal breeding during cultivation, and avoiding chemical finishes, synthetic dyes, heavy metals, residual pesticides, and formaldehyde during manufacturing. They also consider ethical issues that may arise during the production process.

PURE COTTON?

Ordinary cotton is treated with a variety of chemicals as it goes through the processes from plant to fabric, and residues remain even after washing. Choose organic cotton for your bed linen if you want to be sure that you are not breathing in potentially harmful chemicals as you sleep.

TRADITIONAL COTTON VERSUS ORGANIC COTTON | ORGANIC COTTON

	chemicals used	global consequences	health consequences	ORGANIC COTTON
cultivation	▶ Synthetic chemical pesticides and fertilizers that may be highly toxic and cause environmental problems	▶ Chemicals cause decline in soil fertility and erosion ▶ Aerial spraying affects other crops ▶ High water use and water supplies polluted	▶ Traces of chemicals remain and are potentially carcinogenic	▶ **Organic matter fertilizes soil and renews soil productivity** ▶ **Less water used**
harvesting	▶ Herbicides used to defoliate and make picking easier	▶ Chemicals pollute ground and rivers ▶ Harvesting machinery compacts the ground and reduces soil productivity	▶ Traces of chemicals remain and are potentially carcinogenic	▶ **Hand picked (no defoliation, machinery, or chemicals)** ▶ **Hand picking means less waste**
scouring, washing, and bleaching	▶ Chlorine, hydrogen peroxide, APEO (alkylphenoloxylate), EDTA (ethylenediamine tetra-acetate), and VOCs	▶ Synthetic disinfectants are slow to biodegrade ▶ Chlorine emissions pollute atmosphere	▶ Traces of chemicals are carcinogenic and can affect the nervous system	▶ **Natural spinning oils biodegrade easily** ▶ **Natural processing such as potato starch used** ▶ **No chlorine used**
yarn dyeing	▶ Compounds of iron, tin, potassium, and VOCs	▶ Large quantities of water used for washing out dyes ▶ Water polluted by heavy metals	▶ Toxic residues remain	▶ **Natural vegetable dyes or low-impact synthetic dyes; or cotton is color grown**
printing	▶ Solvent-based inks containing heavy metals, benzene, and organochlorides	▶ Waste water is polluted with heavy metals ▶ Emissions form harmful ozone	▶ Toxic residues cause problems of the central nervous system, respiratory system, and skin, as well as headaches, dizziness, and eye irritations	▶ **Natural vegetable and mineral inks and binders are used**
finishing (easycare, stain resistance, fireproofing, mothproofing, softening, deodorizing, anti-static, and mercerizing treatments)	▶ Formaldehyde, caustic soda, sulfuric acid, bromines, urea resins, sulfonamides, halogens, and bromines	▶ Waste water has a high acid content ▶ Emissions to atmosphere	▶ Chemical traces on the fabric can cause burning eyes, nose, and throat, as well as difficulties with sleep, concentration, and memory. Can increase susceptibility to cancer. ▶ Emissions of chemicals from fabric increase with temperature	▶ **No enhancement finishes used**
transportation	In addition to the above, there are environmental consequences of transporting huge quantities of chemicals from the manufacturing plant to the place of cultivation, as well as the additional journeys involved for all stages of cotton production, from the raw material to place of manufacture, finishing, and then to distributor and user.			▶ **Fewer processes so fewer journeys**

FURNITURE

WHEN BUYING FURNITURE, remember the "3Rs" and reduce, repair, and recycle as much as possible. Avoid simply filling space; instead, make sure every piece of furniture fulfills a function. If your home is free of unnecessary items it will appear more spacious, lighter, and generally calmer—and it will be easier to clean.

You can find a wide range of styles of furniture on the market, so avoiding furniture that causes environmental pollution during its production or that damages indoor air quality does not mean a limited choice or having to settle for "rustic" styles. As with so much else today, you have the option of following older traditions that have little impact on the environment or choosing items made by new, clean production methods. Many furniture materials—wood, fabric, plastic, adhesives, and finishes—are discussed elsewhere in this book, but there are a number of aspects discussed in this section that are specific to furniture.

TRADITIONAL HANDCRAFTED FURNITURE

Traditionally handcrafted furniture used natural materials in simple, economic, efficient ways. This approach has produced some of the world's finest furniture—from

SIMPLE ELEGANCE
This simple, elegant furniture *(left),* designed by Alvar Aalto in Finland in the 1930s, combines natural bent beech with canvas fabric.

SHAKER STYLE
Like the Aalto examples, Shaker furniture *(right)* makes the most of natural materials and shapes.

SCULPTURAL FURNITURE

Sculptor Alison Crowther carved this stool *(below)* from a block of locally grown wood. A simple but strikingly beautiful object, it relies on simplicity and the natural color and texture of the wood grain for its effect.

MODERN RECYCLED MATERIALS

Metamorf Design has explored ways of molding recycled thermoplastic material into these lightweight children's chairs *(below)*. The result is highly practical, safe, and fun.

MODERN CRAFTSMANSHIP

This elegant, comfortable dining chair *(above)* is made by the company Trannon, which uses locally grown timber and traditional techniques of craftsmanship.

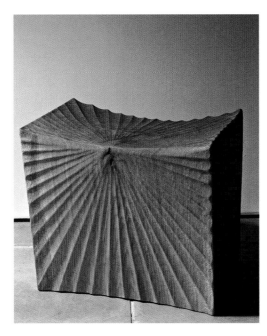

primitive items to the more sophisticated simplicity of Shaker furniture—and it's still equally valid today.

Solid wood furniture is undergoing a renaissance, and designers are developing models based on traditional as well as newer, safe production techniques. Traditionally, the furniture industry relied on the sustained productivity of woodlands achieved by coppicing, which encourages regeneration. Coppicing involves cutting a young tree with a trunk of about 4 inches in diameter, just above ground level, leaving the roots intact. Some 15 years later, new trees have grown from those roots, thus enabling one plant to continue producing usable timber for hundreds of years.

Contemporary designers still use coppiced wood to produce furniture that is spare and light. Long, flexible stalks of willow and ash thinnings can also be woven or bent to create interesting forms for chairs, screens, and stools. Other designers exploit the powerful look of large pieces of unadorned wood to make chunky tables and stools—sometimes boldly plain and other times with delicate surface carvings and softened shapes. Sculptors are also producing carved furniture from huge sections of a log, using the African carving tradition in which a whole item, legs included, is carved from one trunk. This method avoids glues and joints, but it does produce waste. All these designs embody the "less is more" approach and derive their beauty from a simplicity of line and the richness and texture of the wood grain.

When buying wood furniture, check that the wood is certified as ecologically sound: Some retailers advertise these product lines as a marketing aid. In particular, look for products certified by the Forest Stewardship Council (FSC), which can be relied upon to be safe. Even better, select only materials and products that originate locally, thereby avoiding large transportation costs. And remember that the finish on any furniture is just as important as the other materials, so check that finishes and glues used in production are nontoxic (see page 180).

SHAPELY WICKER
This unusual chair *(below)* is
covered with a material made of
environmentally safe, locally grown,
woven grass.

Furniture is also being made from other natural materials such as rushes, rattan, and bamboo. Bamboo is one of the fastest-growing renewable resources and it's also extremely strong and durable. It can be combined with plywood in a composite material for making larger pieces, such as tabletops and work surfaces. Another traditional safe material now being used for interesting designs is made from wood-based paper twine, which is woven into a flexible fabric—sometimes incorporating wire for extra strength—and stretched over a bentwood or cane frame. Such furniture has long been used in the tropics but is becoming universally popular.

RECYCLED FURNITURE AND WASTE MATERIALS
Buying new furniture is not the only way to furnish your home. Many attractive and stylish homes contain long-lasting furniture that has been used before—whether antique or simply secondhand. This approach allows you to select items without constraints of style or period,

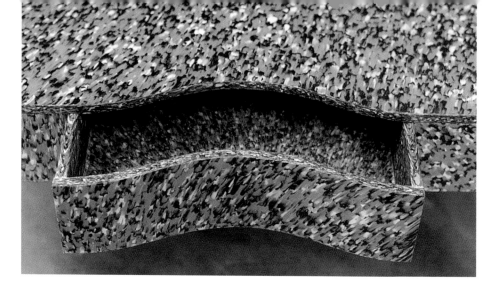

RECYCLED PLASTIC

This tabletop and drawer *(above)* are made from recycled thermoplastic materials such as soft-drink bottles. Like traditional plastic, this material is strong, practical, and easy to clean.

A NEW LOOK

This desk *(right)* by the California company Studio eg is made entirely from recycled materials. The top is recycled plastic, the legs are made from recycled paper tubing, and the feet are recycled rubber. The floor tiles are made of recycled plastic soft-drink bottles.

basing your choice on merit alone. You can find tables, chairs, wardrobes, kitchen cupboards, bathroom vanities, door handles, and windows—anything you can imagine— at salvage yards or secondhand shops. Furnishing in this way demands fewer new products, so it consumes fewer resources and creates less waste.

Recycling waste to make new materials is the foundation of nature's biological processes. By incorporating this principle into manufacturing processes, we can both cope with waste and create materials without consuming more resources. In the United States, reuse of waste is now a significant industry that produces a wide range of materials for making contemporary furniture. Plastic bottles, car tires, waste roofing materials, glass, and aluminum are all reprocessed into new products. Agricultural waste, such as straw, rice, and flax, can be used along with safe glues to make sheet materials to replace unsafe particleboards. Strong panels for furniture are made with light, honeycomb cores in a variety of materials, including recycled aluminium. Paper pulp is an ideal material for smaller items, such as lamp shades, and paper recycled into tubes is being used for table and desk legs.

NEW MATERIALS

Plastics have many advantages: They are cheap, solid, durable, easy to mold and form, and require no surface finishing. However, making plastic endangers the environment, and plastics offgas in our homes. The good news is two types of plastic materials with the same practical advantages are beginning to replace petrochemical plastics. One is made by recycling thermoplastic waste such as bottles; the other uses plant fibers suitable for processing into a plastic substitute.

The first type of new plastic is made from soft-drink bottles that are shredded, then washed and heat-formed into molds or flat sheets. Depending on the process, the waste is either homogenized into a dark charcoal-color material, or the colors of the original waste remain to give a multicolored, flecked appearance. This new plastic has all the advantages of traditional plastic surfaces and laminates and can be used as flat panels or bent into "organic" forms. Office furniture made entirely from recycled plastic and other recycled materials is already available and this type of plastic should soon enter the domestic market. Some of this recycled plastic has been certified safe for use with food, so it's ideal for kitchen worktops.

The second way of making plastic without petrochemicals uses vegetable substances as a base. To date, developments with hemp fiber are giving the best results—it grows well and its long, strong fibers are ideal for processing. There are no polluting emissions, and the resource is renewable and biodegradable. Farmers in Great Britain have been growing hemp for use in car body parts and an Austrian company has developed a hemp-based plastic for molding into a variety of objects such as computer cases, handles, and doorknobs. While growing hemp is banned in the United States, increased awareness of the need for more environmentally sound materials should soon bring hemp-based plastics into the furniture industry

ALUMINUM AND METAL FURNITURE

Metal components are used in furniture to provide strength and durability. All metals come from finite resources and consume energy in production, but more and more metals are being recycled. For example, most aluminum used today has been recycled. While aluminum demands very high-energy input when processed from mined natural bauxite, it lends itself easily to recycling, which uses only 10 percent of the original energy and causes fewer emissions than the original production. The production of primary steel consumes less energy than aluminum, but more energy is needed to recycle the metal. Most steel used in furniture and appliances contains about 50 percent recycled material.

Refinishing treatments can be expensive. While recycled aluminum doesn't need a surface finish, recycled steel

needs to be coated, and many of the most durable coatings (such as chroming and galvanizing) use polluting heavy metals. In addition, paints used on steel are often solvent- or polymer-based, which may be harmful. The increasing reuse of materials means that the environmental consequences of recycling are as important as those associated with primary production. Newer recycling processes are being designed to ensure that they create much less environmental damage.

AIR-FILLED FURNITURE

Perhaps the cleanest, safest, most environmentally friendly furniture of all is that made of air. A major retailer is offering a new range of air-filled chairs and sofas that are a far cry from the uncomfortable, inflatable PVC bubble furniture of the 1970s. The furniture is ergonomically shaped and retains its form because it is made of separate air-filled sections of plastic material. The plastic is so strong that the supplier guarantees to replace any part that may be punctured, free of charge. The inflated item is covered with a comfortable slipcover, available in a range of materials. While the plastic is not benign, it is 100 percent recyclable and the environmental advantages of using so little material to create such a large item are clear.

MASS-PRODUCED PANEL FURNITURE

When labor was cheap and demand could be satisfied by small-scale workshops, furniture of every design was made by craftsmen using safe methods and local materials. But mass-production factories aimed to reduce labor costs, and new fabrication techniques and materials made it possible. Using thin wood veneers, scraps, and particles, sheet materials such as plywood, particleboard, chipboard, and medium-density fiberboard were developed. Today, desks, wardrobes, chests, and kitchen cabinets are assembled from a number of panels of one of

these types of engineered wood, then finished with factory-applied plastic laminate coatings.

While the use of wood waste and sawdust is environmentally sound, these materials are bonded into sheets by adhesives containing formaldehyde and urea resins, which are far from safe. Mass-produced in great quantities throughout the world, engineered-wood furniture is a danger to the atmosphere during manufacture and affects indoor air quality through offgassing. It is far less durable than items made of solid wood and is thrown away after a relatively short life. And although it hasn't been tested, this type of processed board may continue to give off polluting emissions as it degrades.

Another environmentally unsound characteristic of engineered furniture is its smooth, hard-wearing surface. It takes extensive processing to achieve such surfaces, and they are usually finished with high-solvent, plastic-based paints. These processes include gluing plastic laminates under heat with dangerous adhesives, using fillers and bleaches, and spraying of heavy-duty petrochemical paints, transparent stains, or inks. Acetone, ammonia, hydrogen peroxide, and high concentrations of VOCs are commonly emitted during production. In addition, panel furniture is offered in many colors. Every time a color is changed, it involves a huge machine clean-up operation that uses and pollutes large quantities of water.

Panels of engineered wood are normally thin (½ to ¾ inch), and the structural joints in furniture are weak. This means that if the joints break, the panel is damaged and little can be done to repair it. Furthermore, these materials are particularly prone to damage when wet, although stronger water-resistant panels are now becoming available. As a result, countless items such as kitchen units are thrown away, only to be replaced by more particleboard cabinets that differ only in style.

The disadvantages of panel furniture have been recognized, and manufacturing processes are being redesigned to adsorb or incinerate emissions. Replacements are being found for formaldehyde and other unhealthy compounds. Nevertheless, with the bulk of this type of furniture, the worst problems remain.

INDOOR AIR QUALITY

Panel furniture contains resin glues and polymer surface coatings that contribute to poor indoor air. For the first 6 months of their lives, such items offgas significantly, and continue to do so for up to 18 months until they become safe. Dampness, abrasion, and general wear and tear will exacerbate the level of offgassing.

The only way to avoid formaldehyde offgassing is to coat the board with a sealer but, according to the EPA, this is only effective if all surfaces are completely sealed, since

LESS IS MORE

The material in these wire armchairs is used sparingly for an elegant effect—a perfect example of "less is more." The chunky wooden table is equally simple yet effective.

fabrics. Barrier fabrics are safe, synthetic fabrics that are so tightly woven that they prevent dust mites from getting in, yet they are still air permeable.

Allergy sufferers may find it useful to obtain skin-testing kits from specialty fabric suppliers. These kits typically contain all the chemicals used to manufacture the fabric and allow you to test your sensitivity to their product.

FIREPROOFED FURNITURE

Some countries legislate that certain articles of furniture—usually fabric and foam-filled items—should be fireproofed. In the United States, all fireproofed furniture is identified with a label. Fireproofing is generally achieved by coating the item with compounds of bromine, as well as formaldehyde, halogens, and the sulfides of ammonium, zinc, and magnesium, all of which are considered to be health hazards. Ideally, avoid fireproofed items. Instead, choose furniture that does not easily catch fire, and if it should, does not give off dangerous fumes. In many house fires, injury and death are caused not by the fire itself but by inhalation of chemical gases released from plastic foams used in upholstered chairs and sofas. Natural materials such as wood and wool do not pose chemical risk from fire. Wood does not burn easily, but fabrics and paper will be the first items to ignite in a household fire.

It is worth noting that one of the largest and most popular retailers and manufacturers of domestic furniture worldwide has adopted the policy of not fireproofing furniture except where legislation makes it manditory. The best way to make your home safe from fires is to be vigilant and ensure that electric heaters and bare flames from candles and fires are guarded and cannot come into contact with fabrics or paper, even if they should fall. Every home should be fitted with smoke alarms or heat detectors as recommended by your local building inspector.

gases can travel through the material and exit where the coating is missing. To be sure that all surfaces are sealed, you would have to take the furniture apart—generally an impossible task—to reach and check every edge.

Upholstered furniture and beds can harbor dust mites and particulates, which have adverse affects on health, and the fabric can also contain toxic residues. It is healthier to select furniture that is not upholstered or has loose tie-on pads or slipcovers that can be removed for regular washing. Avoid upholstery fillings made of foamed plastic materials that are likely to offgas one of the many chemicals listed on page 180.

It is particularly important to bear these issues in mind when choosing beds and bedding:

▶ Choose a good solid wooden frame bed that is assembled with nontoxic glues and decorated with organic finishes.

▶ Look for a chemical-free mattress made from organic fabric padding and box springs or natural rubber latex. Natural latex is a renewable, safe material and will not harbor dust mites or particulates.

▶ Choose mattress covers, sheets, pillowcases, comforters and duvet covers made of chemical-free cottons or barrier

ENVIRONMENTAL IMPACT OF FURNITURE

✔ GOOD RATING ○ MEDIUM RATING ✗ POOR RATING	resource depletion	energy used[2]	emissions during manufacturing	effect on indoor air	capacity for recycling/ biodegrading
reused furniture[3]	✔	✔	✔	✔	✔
wood[1,3]	✔	✔	✔	✔	✔
particleboard	✔	○	✗	✗	✗
steel	○	✗	✗	✔	○
aluminum[4]	✗	✗	✗	✔	✔
petrochemical plastics	✗	✗	✗	✗	✗
recycled plastics	✔	○	○	○	✔
non-organic natural fabric	○	✗	✗	○	○
organic fabric	✔	✔	✔	✔	✔
synthetic fabric	✗	✗	✗	○	○
new vegetable fibers/plastics	✔	○	✔	✔	✔
bamboo[3]	✔	✔	✔	✔	✔

1. Only sustainable timbers considered.
2. Depends also on distance transported from source to user.
3. Depends on finish.
4. A high proportion of aluminium is now recycled.

FURNITURE TO LOOK FOR

▶ Well-made, long-lasting furniture from local materials that can be repaired if necessary
▶ Furniture made with naturally occurring materials that biodegrade safely
▶ Furniture made from certified woods
▶ Furniture made with wood or metal (aluminum) frames, which is fairly easy to repair
▶ Materials that are solid rather than veneered, finished with traditional oils and waxes that can be renewed at home and improve with age and use
▶ Used furniture or furniture made from recycled materials
▶ Organic fabrics and natural padding and fillings
▶ Soft furnishings that can be removed for washing

FURNITURE TO AVOID

▶ Laminated finishes that are supersmooth; these will become damaged and look worse over time
▶ Particleboard made with urea or formaldehyde glues
▶ Furniture made from tropical hardwoods
▶ Finishes that are high in VOCs and other chemicals
▶ Furniture made from PVC, nylon, and other petroleum-based plastics
▶ Foam- and plastic-filled furniture
▶ Upholstered furniture
▶ Fireproofing that contains bromines, halogens, or formaldehyde
▶ Stain-resistance treatments containing fluorocarbons, PFOs, or formaldehyde
▶ Metal coatings that include chrome, lead, or nickel

RECYCLING

ECYCLING IS ONE OF THE MOST constructive ways to be environmentally safe—provided that the process does not demand so much energy through collection and reprocessing that it cancels any benefits. By recycling—and repairing or reusing—we consume fewer resources and less energy, and generate less waste, thereby reducing our impact on the environment.

Recycling is not a new concept. Generations before us have cherished and repaired things used by their parents and grandparents. Recycling was also a common building practice until the 20th century, when labor became more expensive than materials. This made replacement cheaper than repair but ignored the cost to the earth. Today, a "newer is better" attitude prevails. Ironically, the more new things we buy in pursuit of a supposedly better life, the worse we make the world we live in. Some of the consequences of the "out with the old, in with the new" philosophy have been outlined in Chapter One.

The practice of saving resources through reuse—like so much environmental wisdom—can be found in the design traditions of cultures from all over the world. From a design perspective, what is so striking when looking at these traditions are the imaginative leaps that make creativity with reused materials possible. Like all the most creative ideas, they appear obvious and are often very simple. Examples from traditional cultures are endless—from the reuse over generations of wood, stone, and brick from buildings; of flattened tin drums to make metal roofing or siding; and of copper printing plates transformed into floors. Indigenous peoples have made floors from seashells mixed with lime or fruit stones mixed with blood and dung, while horsehair, dung, and even blood have been combined with lime to plaster and color walls.

The presence of reused materials can create a strong and enjoyable aesthetic—as anyone who has visited ancient Italian or Greek cities (where history lives on in walls made of ancient stones, door surrounds of marble columns, and steps built of old beams) knows. In a more modest way, interiors have this same sense of history when paved with reclaimed stones or built with reused wood or brick. In recent years, the realization that 19th- and early-20th-century buildings have period details that warrant saving for reuse—flooring, flagstones, old boards, brick, fireplaces, doors, windows, and handcrafted decorative moldings—has given rise to commercial enterprises that salvage and resell these objects. Indeed, they are so sought after that a strange inversion of value has developed: Older things, which require no new processing or materials, can be more expensive than the new article. New elements are not in fact cheaper; they are so only because the real costs, the costs to the earth, are not factored in to the cost of their production. But this is changing and environmental concerns and the merits of recycling are beginning to be taken seriously—albeit not quickly enough.

RECYCLING TODAY

U.S. households currently produce 220 million tons of waste per year—which is more than double that of 30 years ago. And only 25 percent is recycled. The Swiss, in contrast, recycle more than 50 percent of their waste. But it is possible to change the way we think about waste. This is being demonstrated by a few far-sighted members of the industrial community, who are beginning to factor into their accounting the true costs of resource depletion, waste, and pollution. More and more products are being manufactured in such a way that they can be easily disassembled so they can be renovated and reused, and manufacturers are recycling waste for their own production processes. It is important to note here that PVC is wholly unsuitable for recycling, despite manufacturers'

RECYCLED STAIRS
Found metal components, bits of machinery and slabs of recycled wood make for a unique sculptural staircase.

claims to the contrary. (For more information on PVC, see page 122.)

Significant social benefits can arise from recycling. Local skills and small businesses in any community have always benefited from being able to repair and reuse items. This is not false idealization of past craftsman-based cultures: It works today in large-scale, commercial economies. In the United States, for example, recycling generates significant employment and revenue for some 73,000 firms, and the number is growing annually.

The message for the homeowner is twofold. First, recycling is environmentally safe; second, the more recycled, environmentally safe products consumers demand, the more manufacturers will offer. Amory Lovins of the Rocky Mountain Institute, the groundbreaking environmental research center, puts it succinctly: "It's remarkable how quickly the phrase, 'Sorry, we don't make that' changes to, 'When do you want it?' when the demand is great enough."

RECYCLING IN THE HOME

A good proportion of any interior can be made from recycled materials and components, which can take a number of forms, as follows:

▶ Reused materials—for example, wood, tiles, and stone
▶ Reused building components—for example, windows, doors, bathroom fixtures and faucets, and fireplaces
▶ Nontraditional materials—for example, straw, newspaper, and salvaged components
▶ Waste items used in different contexts—for example, bottles for walls, cans for curtains or walls, packing cases or pallets for furniture, and cable drums for tables, being careful to avoid those waste materials (such as some

boards) that may have been previously treated with harmful chemicals or preservative sprays

▶ Kitchen waste, wood shavings, wood ash, and similar biodegradable items that can be composted, greatly reducing the amount of waste that goes to landfill sites and increasing the quality of your garden soil

Before you buy anything new, think about whether it can be disassembled and easily repaired, if needed. Select products that have been sturdily made, and choose materials that maintain their good appearance so that you do not have to throw things away simply because they look worse for wear. Although selecting the best may be more expensive in the short term, it will be more economical in the long run. Caring for the environment is not about short-term cost but about long-term saving. If your budget is limited, think quality rather than quantity. A few fine objects in a room will look far more stylish than lots of inferior furniture.

Before throwing something away, ask yourself if it can be repaired, or whether it can be used, in part or entirely, in some other way or for some other function. A broken wooden chair, for example, can be repaired by a local carpenter, or a steel table leg by a local ironworker. Certain "natural" materials lend themselves to repair and this can extend their useful lives. Wood, stone, ceramic tiles, and bricks develop a recognizable and attractive patina that can be very alluring and this is what makes old houses, interiors, furniture, and fixtures so special. They accommodate wear and tear over time—a characteristic that many modern materials do not possess.

A whole world of imaginative and interesting design opportunities opens up when you look at objects and materials around you with a fresh eye to see how they can

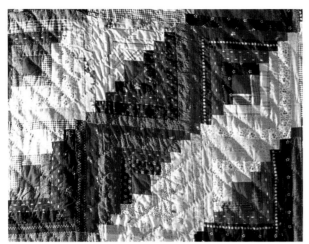

OLD TILES

Ceramic tiles *(above)* can be used time and time again. The patina of age only adds to their attractiveness.

be used in new ways. No idea should be dismissed, however zany—after all, tractor seat stools and washing-machine drums are now design icons. Other ideas include using wooden crates for shelving systems and old railway sleepers, discarded pallets, or even bicycle parts for furniture. Old furniture can also be used in new ways—for example, old cupboards, desks, or dressers can be modified for assembly into kitchen units and worktops. Make chandeliers or mobiles from old compact discs, or fashion partitions from old books within a wood framework. Walls can be decorated with newspapers, maps, and pages from books or even patchworks of old clothes. The attraction of this way of decorating is that it will create totally individual and personal homes that transcend interior design to become almost sculptural interiors unique to their owners. There can be no better way of saving resources.

But designing with cast-offs needs care in order to prevent your space from looking like a chaotic assembly of what you happen to have found. Traditional American patchwork quilts demonstrate the key to making a beautiful whole from many disparate elements—a strong design organizes the many scraps into a whole. Far from being a limitation, an ordered approach will be a springboard for creativity and ingenuity. For example, when reusing floorboards from different sources or of inadequate lengths, turn this to design advantage by using the boards in a herringbone pattern, or form a pattern of short boards laid perpendicular to a grid of long boards. Even if you lay boards lengthways as normal there is no need to have consistent board widths or lengths—equal boards derive from mass manufacture and a need for speed in laying. Some of the finest traditional floors are made from random widths and lengths, and they are coveted today for their character and charm.

Similarly, when using recycled windows or similar components of different sizes, you may be happy with the haphazard look, or you can organize them by arranging them into a regular grid or framework, again enjoying the interplay of regular and irregular patterns.

The same approach can be used when recycling tiles for floors or walls, where an overall ordering geometry is also important. You can create attractive borders or patterns using different types of tiles, or even broken pieces.

NEW MATERIALS

Exploring new materials made from "trash" can offer exciting opportunities for designers. This comfortable armchair designed by Lothar Windels *(above)* is made from wool recycled into thick felt. Over time, the felt gradually adjusts to fit the shape of your body.

Combine large areas of plain concrete floors or plaster walls, with patterns of broken tiles or glass. The Spanish architect Gaudi and the sculptor Andrew Logan have created sumptuous designs for walls and furniture using broken tiles, glass, and mirror work. Developing such designs will give your interior a personality unlike any other and be infinitely more delightful than even the most expensive new surface covering.

NEW MATERIALS AND CLEAN PRODUCTION

In the past, many practical devices were made by hand from wood, clay, or other naturally occurring materials. This is no longer the case for so much of what we use today. But it is, in fact, in this sphere of mass production that we are now on a threshold of opportunity for large-scale recycling. The growth of closed-loop processes, or biomimicry (see page 30), offers the potential to develop the most advanced materials, avoiding the environmental damage of dirty industrial processes (see page 30). Companies such as Interface and Milliken—both carpet manufacturers—IBM, Sony, Gramme GMBH, and BMW, are moving toward being able to supply new products

RECYCLED KITCHEN

A discarded iron grill from a subway station was rescued to make a hanging pot rack *(above)*. Nearly all of this kitchen, designed by architect Pedro Guedes, has been made from recycled waste.

Sixty layers of recycled corrugated cardboard are folded to create strength in this unusual dining chair by Frank Gehry *(left)*. The trim is made of recycled fiberboard.

INTEGRAL PATTERNS

Careful sorting of the materials used to make recycled plastic can create interesting patterns *(below)*.

made almost entirely from waste and recycled materials or materials from new "clean" processes. This applies to technologically sophisticated items such as cars and computers, as well as to more basic items like engineered wood for floors, and furniture, fabrics, and paints. Designers—mainly in the United States and northern Europe—are marketing stunning ranges of furniture made from recycled plastic; an attractive range of artificial fiber fleece throws are made from plastic soft-drink bottles; a Spanish company is developing exquisite chairs using almond shells; and crushed light bulbs and mussel shells are being used to make floor and wall tiles.

Previously unexploited materials from vegetable sources are also coming into use. Hemp, for example, is now recognized as offering enormous potential, not only for fabric fibers but also for making plasticlike substances (see page 157). Of particular interest to designers and decorators are new, sustainable, woodlike products such as bamboo. Programs are under way to find uses for the vast numbers of palms that are cultivated throughout the world for their fruit, but that have a relatively short productive life. Coconut palm wood, for example, is proving

to be a useful and durable alternative to wood, but inadequate marketing has limited its availability. But material from the pejibella and concha fruiting palms of Central America is now under construction. This beautiful material is ebony colored with light flashes, and is exceptionally durable and tough. Such materials offer interesting and unique design possibilities that are also environmentally safe. While they are not yet readily available, you should look out for them as their availability will grow. Consider at the same time, however, the energy used for transportation, as well as the ethical issues that come into play when using imported products in your home. There is always a strong environmental case for buying local products when you have a choice.

NEW PATTERNS OF TRADE

Imaginative thinking about consumption patterns and resource inefficiency is leading to new, safer economic models. For example, instead of selling you a washing machine, a company in Chicago will loan you one, free of charge. It will service, repair, or replace the machine when needed, simply charging you every time you wash your clothes. Instead of consumers buying, using, throwing out, and then buying new machines, the company uses its expertise to reuse and recycle the same equipment for as long as each component will function. This model, which is also developing in the commercial carpet industry, rests on the same logic used by city-dwellers who are beginning to reject the car that stands idle for 22 out of 24 hours, and instead renting a car or using a taxi when they need one.

DOWNCYCLING

A new approach to recycling called downcycling is being developed alongside new, clean industrial processes. This involves salvaging discarded objects and materials no longer suitable for use in their original form and reprocessing them into the ingredients of new materials for

COLORFUL PLASTIC

COLORFUL PLASTIC
Recycled materials need not be dull, as is
evident from this plastic material *(below)*
that incorporates bold, vivid colors.

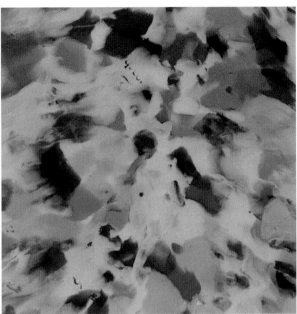

other uses. This is not something the householder can do,
but you should be aware that such products are beginning
to come onto the market—and choose them, when appropriate. Examples include shredding paper to use as insulating material or in lampshades, and grinding up plastics
to produce the material to make plastic furniture, door-
mats, and carpets. Attractive glass objects are made from
recycled glass, while some rubber flooring contains a high
percentage of used car tires.

This new and radical reorientation of industrial production and consumption has at its heart the traditional
wisdom of harboring resources and designing with, rather
than against, nature. This offers designers and home-
makers exciting opportunities and the acceptance of a
much broader approach to style. In this way, environmental concerns, far from being limiting, provide the springboard to create exciting and attractive homes that display
imagination and a unique, personal style.

Chapter Four

HEALTHY HOME DIRECTORY

GOING FURTHER

AT THE OUTSET OF THIS BOOK, I accepted that interior decoration and home furnishings play a small part in a home's impact on the environment, compared to its construction and energy efficiency. A fully sustainable home would be heated entirely by casual heat gains (from our bodies, cooking, appliances, solar heating, and so on). It would use only collected and recycled water, compost all waste, and be free from almost all harmful emissions or materials. Ideally every home would be sustainable, but this can be possible only through wholesale changes to construction and service installations.

Such changes are beyond the scope of most homeowners—and beyond the scope of this book. However, I hope that by showing that an environmental approach to design can make attractive and satisfying interiors, you may be spurred on to take more far-reaching actions toward making a sustainable home.

The following lists outline ideas that can help you improve the overall performance of your home. The environmental principles outlined in Chapter One—the use of as few resources as possible, minimum energy use, minimum emissions and waste, and maximum biodegradability—should guide all the decisions about construction. For instance, the more efficient you make the thermal insulation and service installations (such as heat and electricity) in your home, the greater your home's energy efficiency will be. But this does not mean that major construction is the only way to improve efficiencies. One of the easiest ways to gain energy savings is to add good attic insulation. Which of the ideas listed will be the most energy saving or cost effective for you will depend upon the location and construction of your home.

RENEWABLE ELECTRICITY

More and more companies are selling electricity generated from renewable sources. The most common sources are wind, solar, and hydroelectric, but biomass, biogas, geothermal, and wave power are also beginning to be used. The availability of renewable sources differs widely. You will need to explore suppliers in your area to see what alternative sources are available where you live. While you'll need to decrease your overall energy use to realize a cost savings, simply changing to a cleaner, renewable source of electricity will help save our earth's resources.

You can find additional information on energy savings in other books and pamphlets and through organizations that encourage and assist in energy efficiency. A selection is listed on page 182. The Internet is another excellent source of information ranging from the highly theoretical to practical installation advice. Most local government offices also offer advice.

John Broome's modern design accentuates
natural resources, such as sunlight and green
plants, and uses them to their best advantage.

REDUCING ENERGY CONSUMPTION

▶ Increase the thermal insulation of
walls, roofs, and floors, as well as
doors and windows.

▶ Use wind shelters, fences, walls,
trees, and hedges to shelter your
building from prevailing winds and
reduce heat loss.

▶ Locate bathrooms on outside walls
so that you can ventilate them
directly to the outside and minimize
the use of internal fans.

▶ Change the type of fuel you use
to the most efficient available in
your area.

▶ Construct additions to take
advantage of maximum solar gain by
orienting them toward the sun.

▶ If you have a conservatory or sun
room, make sure that it can be
isolated from adjacent living areas so
that you don't lose heat in winter.

▶ Recover heat from waste water by
using a heat pump.

▶ Generate your own power from
renewable sources such as solar
water heating, photoelectric cells,
wind power, and heat pumps.

REDUCING HEAT LOSS

▶ Weather-strip windows and doors.

▶ Seal all joints between elements—
window to wall, roof to pipe and
cable entry points, etc.

▶ Control all unregulated drafts.

▶ Add air locks to all external doors.

SAVING WATER AND REDUCING SOLID WASTE

▶ Install a water-saving toilet.

▶ Install showers rather than baths.

▶ When installing a water-heating
system, centralize the plumbing to
minimize the length of your hot-
water pipes.

▶ Install a rainwater collection
system to supply toilets and for use
in garden hoses.

▶ Install an approved gray-water
system that reuses water from sinks
and baths and recycles it for watering
your landscaping.

▶ Install composting toilets.

▶ When adding on to your home, do
as much construction as possible with
recycled building products.

▶ Don't throw away used or unused
building materials; recycle them.

ELECTRICAL APPLIANCES

ENERGY STAR LABEL

ENERGY STAR-labeled products use less energy than other products, save you money on utility bills, and help protect the environment. You can find the ENERGY STAR label on quality household appliances, home electronics, office equipment, heating and cooling equipment, windows, residential light fixtures, and more. ENERGY STAR products are made by all the major manufactures, are and sold by retailers everywhere.

USING ENERGY-EFFICIENT APPLIANCES can significantly reduce your home's consumption of electricity. A household equipped with all the most efficient appliances available would consume only one-third of the electricity used by one with the most inefficient appliances. Choosing energy-efficient models is particularly important with appliances that are permanently turned on, such as refrigerators and freezers. In many countries these appliances alone consume almost as much electricity as all the office buildings combined. Televisions and videos on standby mode are also permanently "on" and waste energy. If all the televisions in the United States were left on standby, they would use as much power as the Chernobyl nuclear power station.

Selecting energy-efficient appliances is good for your pocket as well as good for the earth. They may be more expensive to buy initially, but this will be offset by savings in fuel—particularly if fuel costs rise. Although good practice normally encourages the long-term use of goods, this does not apply to old electrical appliances. The latest efficient appliances consume so much less energy that it is better to discard old inefficient models and buy new ones. Furthermore, governments and electricity suppliers sometimes subsidize the cost of energy-efficient machines as part of their commitment to energy saving. When buying top-rated appliances, you get a much better model than you are paying for. Guidance for purchasers exists in the form of energy-efficiency labels that rate products from A to G. In the United States, look for the Energy Star certification and Energy Guide labels.

Appliances have other environmental impacts; for example, water and detergent use in washers are also assessed on the label. The noise level of an appliance may also appear on the label. For complete information about an applicance, consult the manufacturer's literature or ask the retailer. When buying and using electric appliances, take the following issues into account.

GENERAL GUIDELINES

▶ When choosing appliances, consider the amount of energy it will consume during use rather than in production, since this will have the greater environmental impact. Look for and read carefully energy-efficiency labels.

▶ Choose gas appliances whenever possible. They use less energy, are cheaper to run than electrical models, and produce fewer emissions. Have them checked regularly to avoid the risk of carbon monoxide poisoning.

▶ Keep all appliances well maintained to increase their

efficiency: Defrost refrigerators and freezers, clean the coils behind refrigerators, and unblock filters in washers and vents in dryers.

▶ Don't rely on energy-saving plugs. They appear to work only on older appliances.

▶ Choose the smallest appliance that suits your needs.

▶ Run appliances during off-peak hours (but be aware of any noise that might disturb neighbors). With many electricity companies, off-peak electricity is not only cheaper but also uses power that is more efficiently generated than peak-time electricity.

▶ Dispose of equipment at proper recycling stations. Take refrigerators to certified locations because of their dangerous refrigerant gases.

COOKING APPLIANCES

▶ If you use an electric stove, choose the most efficient cooking elements. The best types are induction burners, followed by ceramic burners and ring elements. Solid disc hot plates are the least efficient.

▶ Use a jug-style kettle to boil only the amount of water needed. Boiling water on a gas stove uses less energy than using an electric kettle.

REFRIGERATORS AND FREEZERS

▶ Select a refrigerator that has natural gas rather than HFC

refrigerants. Check with the manufacturer.

▶ Make sure that there is adequate ventilation around your refrigerator and freezer. A poorly ventilated refrigerator can use as much as 90 percent more energy.

▶ Don't place a refrigerator or freezer next to a stove or other hot appliance. It will have to work harder and consume more energy.

▶ Set your refrigerator and freezer to the highest temperature at which they will work efficiently. Some models have special eco-settings.

▶ Special features are expensive to run: Icemaking consumes up to 25 percent and auto-defrost up to 40 percent additional electricity.

▶ Use a cold cellar if you have one to store as many foods as possible so you can get by with a smaller refrigerator.

WASHING MACHINES AND DISHWASHERS

▶ Buy a washing machine with a horizontal-axis clothes drum rather than a tub type. They use less energy and less water, and they are gentler on clothes.

▶ Wash clothes and dishes at the lowest possible temperatures—104°F rather than 140°F is adequate, except for removing oil and grease stains.

▶ Locate washing machines and dishwashers as close to the hot water source as possible

▶ Always run machines on full loads.

▶ Dry clothes on a line whenever possible.

▶ Choose a ventilating clothes dryer; they're more efficient than condensing dryers.

TELEVISIONS, AUDIO EQUIPMENT, AND COMPUTERS

▶ Never leave a television, video, or stereo in standby mode. It remains permanently on, and the total electricity used can amount to 80 percent more than that used when the machine is actually in use.

▶ If you have equipment with transformers, turn off the transformer as well as the appliance when you're not using it.

▶ When replacing small appliances such as battery chargers, outdoor path lights, burglar alarms, and doorbells, choose solar-powered versions. None will make a great difference to the total energy consumption of your home, but every little bit helps.

▶ Keep your computer equipment, particularly the monitor, switched off when not in use. If it is essential to keep equipment on standby, the "sleep" or "energy-save" mode takes only 10 percent of the energy consumed by leaving it fully on.

▶ Manufacturing computers is highly energy intensive. If possible, choose a manufacturer who recycles computer parts.

ECO-LABELING

NCREASING UNDERSTANDING OF THE IMPORTANCE of environmental issues has prompted a flurry of products that are supposedly environmentally sound entering the market. Many manufacturers use meaningless terms such as "environmentally friendly" or "kind to nature" without substantiating these claims. But consumer concern has also given rise to independent organizations that assess and certify whether products are truly ecologically sound and sustainable. Although a universal standard is impossible for all products everywhere, eco-labels identify the extent to which a product is designed and manufactured to have the minimum environmental impact. Some eco-label programs are government funded. Others charge manufacturers for assessing their products. The downside of this is that equally safe products from smaller companies may be excluded simply because of the cost.

The criteria used in labeling programs vary from organization to organization, but all broadly consider the issues covered in this book:

▶ Resource depletion
▶ Energy demand
▶ Avoiding chemicals in manufacture
▶ Avoiding chemical emissions, residues, and offgassing
▶ Biodegradability
▶ Ethical issues

The 24- to 26-member Global Eco-Labeling Network attempts to coordinate standards worldwide and publicizes all assessments from their member organizations. You can find these assessments on the Internet at www.gen.gr.jp.

Ethical and fair-trade issues are usually covered by separate certifying organizations. Rugmark, for example, ensures that rugs are ethically made without enforced or child labor and that companies pay proper wages and sponser children's educational programs. Claims by retailers and suppliers that their products are safe and ethically produced (although uncertified) should be viewed with some skepticism, since there is little that the consumer can do to verify such claims. Energy labeling programs measure only the energy efficiency of an appliance in use and, where appropriate, its water consumption. In the United States, look for the Energy Star label (see page 176).

From the point of view of the typical consumer, looking for eco-labels is probably the most realistic way to shop for the most environmentally safe products, and you'll see a selection of the most common ones here. Other than that, you can subject each product to your own assessment according to the issues outlined in this book. Manufacturers are increasingly posting details of their products on the Internet, which is a valuable source of information.

GREEN SEAL (UNITED STATES)
Independent, nonprofit organization that certifies and publishes recommendations on products, including paint, windows, cleaning products, and appliances.

ENVIRONMENTAL CHOICE (CANADA)
Certifies a wide range of domestic products, including appliances, paints, adhesives, carpets, and building materials.

FOREST STEWARDSHIP COUNCIL

Worldwide certification program for wood and wood-derived products, including engineered wood and wallpaper.

RUGMARK

Certifies that carpet or rug has been produced without illegal child labor.

USA CARPET INDUSTRY "GREEN LABEL" PROGRAM

Voluntary code for carpets with low chemical content. Some British manufacturers also adhere to this standard.

SCIENTIFIC CERTIFICATION SYSTEMS

Neutral third-party certification since 1984 for a wide variety of environmental and food safety claims, including Environmental Preferability, Recycled Content, Biodegradability, Poison-Free, No Ozone Depleting Chemicals, Well-Managed Forests (accredited by the Forest Stewardship Council), Well-Managed Fisheries (accredited by the Marine Stewardship Council), NutriClean No Detected Pesticide Residues, Organic, and CertiClean HACCP food safety management.

NUTRICLEAN

Certifies food meeting a strict "No Detected Pesticide Residue" standard for organic and conventionally grown foods. Division of Scientific Certification Systems.

CHEMICALS

NO LIST CAN IDENTIFY EVERY DANGEROUS CHEMICAL. Nor is it the case that the presence of the chemicals listed will automatically make you ill—the extent to which they affect us depends on our age, general health, and living environment. All that I aim to do here is to increase awareness and identify the worst and most commonly found dangers. Listed at right are common chemicals that should be avoided, which are found in paints, adhesives, and many plastics. Many of them have a number of different names, some of which are given in parentheses. These chemicals are identified in a number of registers, including the Green Seal testing program (see page 178), as known or possible carcinogens or environmental pollutants.

Chemicals are used not only for primary functions, such as to provide color or adhesion, but also for less obvious purposes such as binding, dispersing, filling, softening, hardening, and plasticising, and as antifoaming and bactericidal agents. Even more chemicals are needed to ensure that all these ingredients combine and work together. By contrast, organic products contain only naturally occurring ingredients that are generally compatible with our biological systems.

It is impossible to list the health consequences of all chemicals. They can range from mild effects such as headaches and respiratory irritations to more serious conditions such as asthma, reproductive problems, and cancers. Chemicals can also have behavioral and performance consequences ranging from mild to severe cases of fatigue, irritability, memory impairment, inability to concentrate, and mood disorders. Environmental effects include polluting emissions to air, land, and water; photochemical smog; and ozone depletion.

When choosing products for your home, take time to consider the safety of the ingredients as well as their visual and practical aspects. Use materials that are as close as possible to their natural state and have the fewest chemical ingredients, unless there is an overriding reason not to do so. Be particularly careful to check the ingredients of materials used in kitchens, bedrooms, and children's rooms, particularly if you're preparing a room for a new baby. Also take extra care when choosing materials that are likely to get scuffed or become hot or wet—such conditions will make them more likely to release their toxic ingredients. Remember to check the adhesives used with materials, too. Choose those that don't contain borax, formaldehyde, halogenated solvents, heavy metals, or more than 5 percent VOC solvents.

There are millions of chemicals in use today. This list isn't exhaustive, nor does the omission of any chemical in any way imply it is safe. For more on chemicals, refer to "Sources" on page 182 or "Bibliography" on page 191.

- ▶ 1,1,1–Trichlorethane (TCE)
- ▶ Benzene and benzyl chlorides
- ▶ Ethylbenzine (EB)
- ▶ Toluene
- ▶ Vinyl chloride (VCM)
- ▶ Naphthalene
- ▶ 1,2–Dichlorobenzene
- ▶ Phthalates (DEHP, BEHP, and DOP)
- ▶ Formaldehyde (methal aldehyde, methal oxides, formalin)
- ▶ Methyl ethyl ketone (MEK)
- ▶ Acrolien (acrylaldehyde, propenol, ethylene aldehyde)
- ▶ Acrylonitrile (vinyl cyanide, or VCN)
- ▶ N-butyl alcohol
- ▶ Acetic aldehydes
- ▶ Chlorofluorocarbons (CFCs)
- ▶ Dichlorobenzines
- ▶ Methyl naphthalene
- ▶ Chlorotoluene
- ▶ White spirit (aliphatic hydrocarbons)
- ▶ Xylene
- ▶ Methyline chloride (dichloromethane)
- ▶ Antimony
- ▶ Cadmium
- ▶ Lead
- ▶ Mercury
- ▶ Styrenes (Phenylethelene, vinyl benzine)
- ▶ Polyuretheanes
- ▶ Polyisocianates
- ▶ Naphtha
- ▶ Propylene
- ▶ Methanol
- ▶ Ethanol
- ▶ Propylene glycol and oxide (epoxy propane)
- ▶ Ethylene glycol and ethelyne oxide
- ▶ Halogenated hydrocarbons

CHECKLIST

Y OU CAN MAKE LOTS OF CHANGES AROUND your home that don't require any major building work or disruptions to your routine. Use this handy checklist to help you get started.

APPLIANCES AND LIGHTS

▶ Buy energy-efficient appliances.
▶ Use dishwashers and washing machines only at full capacity.
▶ Don't keep a refrigerator running for only a few items.
▶ Select long-lasting equipment and items that could be repaired if needed.
▶ Service all equipment, particularly microwaves, regularly.
▶ Use low-energy light bulbs.
▶ Use sensors or timers so that hallway or outdoor lights are not left on when not needed.
▶ Never use the standby option on your television and audio equipment.
▶ Use solar-powered versions of small appliances such as battery chargers, doorbells, and alarms.
▶ Keep 3 feet away from electrical appliances if possible.
▶ Have all gas appliances serviced and tested regularly for carbon monoxide emissions.

HEATING AND ENERGY CONSUMPTION

▶ Reduce the peak temperature on your home heating system.
▶ Use thermostats and programmable controls to control heat, and follow patterns of use rather than keeping water or rooms heated when not needed.

▶ Reduce the temperature of hot water for bathing (maximum 130°F) and for washing clothes and dishes (maximum 105°F).
▶ Reduce the amount of hot water you store. Combine furnaces for heating water with home heating.
▶ Locate heat sources for maximum efficiency and put reflectors behind radiators on outside walls.
▶ Use radiant panel heaters (see page 70) wherever possible.
▶ Draftproof your home and increase insulation, particularly in attics, but make sure there is adequate ventilation.
▶ Install passive ventilation devices (see page 78) instead of electric fans.
▶ Maximize solar heat gain.
▶ Buy electricity from suppliers that generate power from renewable sources.

MATERIALS AND FURNISHINGS

▶ Use as few applied finishes as possible, and let the natural look of a material speak for itself.
▶ Select sturdy pieces of furniture that will last a long time.
▶ Repair and extend the useful life of as many things as possible.
▶ Use local materials and suppliers.
▶ Choose naturally occurring, organic, biodegradable materials.

▶ If you do need chemically based products, try to avoid those chemicals listed opposite.
▶ Use recycled items.
▶ Choose products made in closed-loop processes (see page 30).
▶ Buy from ethical producers whenever possible.
▶ Avoid using materials in short supply or from protected resources.
▶ If possible, choose products that are certified by a reputable eco-labeling organization (see page 178).

SAVING WATER AND REDUCING WASTE

▶ Take showers rather than baths.
▶ Don't install water-hungry power showers.
▶ Put a brick in your toilet tank to save water when flushing.
▶ Collect rainwater in barrels for watering your lawn or garden.
▶ Buy as few packaged goods as possible.
▶ Recycle as much solid waste as you can: paper, cardboard, aluminium, steel, glass, and plastics.
▶ Compost all biodegradable kitchen waste.
▶ Take used appliances and furniture to repair and reuse organizations.
▶ Take small household objects and clothes to secondhand shops.

SOURCES

ADVISORY ORGANIZATIONS ON HEALTH AND ENVIRONMENTAL ISSUES

Alliance to End Childhood Lead Poisoning

227 Massachusetts Avenue NE
Suite 200
Washington, DC 20002
Phone: (202) 543-1147
Web site: www.aeclp.org
Lead paint removal information

Children's Health Environmental Coalition (CHEC)

PO Box 1540
Princeton, NJ 08542
Phone: (609) 252-1915
Fax: (609) 252-1536
E-mail: chec@checnet.org
Web site: www.checnet.org
Nonprofit research organization that examines causes of childhood cancers

Environmental Defense (formerly Environmental Defense Fund)

257 Park Avenue South
New York, NY 10010
Phone: (800) 684-3322
Fax: (212) 505-2575
Web site: www.environmentalde
   fense.org
A not-for-profit environmental advocacy group with four main goals: stabilizing the Earth's climate, safeguarding the world's oceans, protecting human health, and defending and restoring biodiversity

Environmental Working Group

1718 Connecticut Avenue NW
Suite 600
Washington, DC 20009
Web site: www.ewg.org
A leading content provider for public interest groups and concerned citizens who are campaigning to protect the environment

U.S. Department of Labor

OSHA (Occupational Safety and
   Health Organization)
Office of Public Affairs–Room N3647
200 Constitution Avenue
Washington, DC 20210
Phone: (202) 693-1999
Web site: www.osha.gov
Government agency regulating safety and health standards in the workplace

U.S. Environmental Protection Agency (EPA)

Ariel Rios Building
1200 Pennsylvania Avenue NW
Washington, DC 20460
Phone: (202) 260-2090
Web site: www.epa.gov
U.S. governmental agency, comprehensive source for information on environmental safety issues

INFORMATION ON NEW CLEAN TECHNOLOGY

Rocky Mountain Institute

1739 Snowmass Creek Road
Snowmass, CO 81654-9199
Phone: (970) 927-3851
An entrepreneurial, nonprofit organization that fosters the efficient and restorative use of resources to create a more secure, prosperous, and life-sustaining world

United Nations Environment Program

Regional Office for North America
1707 H Street NW
Suite 300
Washington, DC 20006
Phone: (202) 785-0465
Fax: (202) 785-2096 or 785-4871
Web site: www.unep.org
Worldwide programs provide leadership and encourage partnership in caring for the environment by inspiring, informing, and enabling nations and peoples to improve their quality of life without compromising that of future generations

INFORMATION ON CHEMICALS AND POLLUTANTS

Greenpeace

702 H Street NW
Washington, DC 20001
Phone: (800) 326-0959
Web site: www.greenpeace.org
International organization battling chemical pollution and environmental threats throughout the world

International Agency for Research on Cancer (IARC)

150 cours Albert Thomas
F-69372 Lyon cedex 08, France
Phone: 33 (0)4 72 73 84 85
Fax: 33 (0)4 72 73 85 75
Part of the World Health Organization, IARC's mission is to coordinate and conduct research on the causes of human cancer and the mechanisms of carcinogenesis, and to develop scientific strategies for cancer control. The agency is involved in both epidemiological and laboratory research and disseminates scientific information through publications, meetings, courses, and fellowships.

National Coalition against the Misuse of Pesticides

701 E Street SE
#200
Washington, DC 20003
Phone: (202) 543-5450
Fax: (202) 543-4791
Web site: www.beyondpesticides.org

A nonprofit organization that serves as a national network committed to pesticide safety and adoption of alternative pest management strategies

Seventh Generation

One Mill Street
Box A26
Burlington, VT 05401-1530
Phone: (802) 658-3773
Fax: (802) 658-1771
Web site: www.seventhgen.com

Supplier of domestic and building products with a database of information on chemicals and pollution

U.S. Consumer Product Safety Commission

Washington, DC 20207-0001
Phone: (800) 638-2772
Web site: www.cpsc.gov

An independent federal regulatory agency that helps keep American families safe by reducing the risk of injury or death from consumer products. Extensive database on chemicals and indoor air quality, including issues of safety in the home.

INFORMATION ON ENVIRONMENTAL BUILDING TECHNIQUES AND MATERIALS

Center for Resourceful Building Technology

PO Box 100
Missoula, MT 59806
Phone: (406) 549-7678
Fax: (406) 549-4100
E-mail: crbt@ncat.org
Web site: www.crbt.org

Identifies and promotes building products and methods that do more with less; that provide building materials from reused, salvaged, underutilized, or waste materials; that provide sufficient housing with reduced resource use; and that produce less pollution and waste than conventional building materials and technologies

Environmental Building News

122 Birge Street
Suite 30
Brattleboro, VT 05301
Phone: (802) 257-7300
Fax: (802) 257-7304
Web site: www.buildinggreen.com

Newsletter focused on environmentally responsible design and construction; provides source lists of products and services

The Green Design Network

Web site: www.greendesign.net

Searchable Internet database of more than 600 sites related to environmentally conscious design and construction

Sustainable Buildings Industry Council (SBIC)

1331 H Street NW
Suite 1000
Washington, DC 20005
Phone: (202) 628-7400
Fax: (202) 393-5043
Web site: www.sbicouncil.org

A national resource for sustainable design and product information, SBIC provides accurate, easy-to-use guidelines, software, and general information about energy conservation measures, energy efficient equipment and appliances, daylighting, and sustainable architecture

U.S. Green Building Council

1015 18th Street NW
Suite 805
Washington, DC 20036
Phone: (202) 828-7422
Fax: (202) 828-5110
Web site: www.usgbc.org

The mission of this unprecedented coalition is to accelerate the adoption of green building practices, technologies, policies, and standards

ALTERNATIVE ENERGY ORGANIZATIONS

The American Solar Energy Society (ASES)

2400 Central Avenue
Suite G-1
Boulder, CO 80301
Phone: (303) 443-3130
Fax: (303) 443-3212
E-mail: ases@ases.org
Web site: www.ases.org

A national organization dedicated to advancing the use of solar energy for the benefit of U.S. citizens and the global environment

American Wind Energy Association

122 C Street NW
Suite 380
Washington, DC 20001
Phone: (202) 383-2500
Fax: (202) 383-2505
E-mail: windmail@awea.org
Web site: www.awea.org

Advocates development of wind energy as a reliable, environmentally sound energy alternative

Global Energy Marketplace

Web site: http://gem.crest.org

A gateway to sustainable energy information on the Web.

RECYCLING AND SALVAGE

Global Recycling Network

Brookhaven, NY 11719
Fax: (631) 286-8471
Web site: www.grn.com

A free-access public site dedicated to recycling-related information, including profiles of companies using recycled materials

The Internet Consumer Recycling Guide

Web site: www.obviously.com

This Web site provides a starting point for consumers in the United States and Canada searching the Internet for recycling information. The information is for people with regular household quantities of materials to recycle.

Salvaged Building Materials Exchange

Web site: www.greenguide.com

Part of a larger green building Web site, this resource lets you seek sources for, or sell your own, recycled building materials

ETHICAL TRADE

Ethical Consumer Magazine

Unit 21, 41 Old Birley Street
Manchester UK M15 5RF
Phone: 0044-0161-226-2929
Fax: 0044-0161-226-6277
E-mail: ethicon@mcr1.poptel.org.uk
Web site: www.ethicalconsumer.org

Fairtrade Labeling Organizations International

Kaiser Friedrich Strasse 13
53113 Bonn Germany
Phone: +49-228-949230
Web site: www.fairtrade.net

A group that monitors production of various foods to ensure that they meet fair labor criteria

ECO-LABELING ORGANIZATIONS

CRI (Carpet and Rug Institute) USA

Phone: (800) 882-8846

Environment Canada

45 Alderney Drive
Dartmouth, Nova Scotia B2Y 2N6
 Canada
Phone: (902) 426-7231
Fax: (902) 426-6348
Web site: www.ns.ec.gc.ca

Promotes environmental programs and behaviors

Forest Stewardship Council–U.S.

1134 29th Street NW
Washington, DC 20007
Phone: (877) 372-5646
Fax: (202) 342-6589
Web site: www.fscus.org

The Forest Stewardship Council certifies companies that use wood products from sustainably managed forests. FSC-endorsed forests are managed in an ecologically sound, socially responsible, and economically viable manner.

Global Ecolabeling Network

TerraChoice Environmental Services, Inc.
2781 Lancaster Road
Suite 400
Ottawa, Ontario K18 147 Canada
Web site: www.gen.gr.jp

A nonprofit association of eco-labeling organizations from around the world

Green Seal

1001 Connecticut Avenue NW
Suite 827
Washington, DC 20036-5525
Phone: (202) 872-6400
Fax: (202) 872-4324
Web site: www.greenseal.org

Independent nonprofit organization that sets environmental standards and awards seals of approval to products that meet those standards

Rugmark

733 15th Street NW
Suite 920
Washington, DC 20005
Phone: (202) 347-4205
Fax: (202) 347-4885
E-mail: info@rugmark.org
Web site: www.rugmark.org

Certifies that carpet has been made without illegal child labor

Scientific Certification Systems

1939 Harrison Street
Suite 400
Oakland, CA 94612
Phone: (510) 832-1415
Fax: (510) 832-0359
Web site: www.scs1.com

Third-party certifier for testing multiple facets of food industry, including pesticide residue on fresh produce

PRODUCT SUPPLIERS

Breathefree.com, Inc.

12611 Hidden Creek Way
Suite E
Cerritos, CA 90703
Phone: (888) 434-8313
Web site: www.breathefree.com

HEPA filter vacuums, freestanding humidifiers, humidifiers that attach to furnaces, electronic air cleaners with HEPA filters

EcoMall

Web site: www.ecomall.com

A Web directory of environmentally friendly organizations and businesses

Web site: www.enviresource.com

Direct retailer of environmentally friendly flooring, paint and finishes, lumber, bedding, linens, etc.

Environmental Home Center

1724 Fourth Avenue S
Seattle, WA 98134
Phone: (206) 682-7332 or
   (800) 281-9785
Fax: (206) 682-8275
Web site: www.enviresource.com

EnviroSource.com, Inc.

1523 North Pascal Street
Suite 100
St. Paul, MN 55108-2328
Phone: (651) 645-0294
E-mail: info@envirosource.com
Web site: www.envirosource.com

An electronic enviro-mall that includes an e-store and links to environmental product suppliers, contractors, and organizations

The Green Culture

PO Box 1684
Laguna Beach, CA 92652
Phone: (800) 233-8438
Web site: www.greenculture.com

Nontoxic pest and rodent control

Harmony

360 Interlocken Boulevard
Broomfield, CO 80021
Phone: (800) 456-1177
Web site: www.gaiam.com

Seventh Generation cleaning products, anti-allergy sprays and powders, HEPA air filters and vacuums, fans

Healthy Home Center

1403-A Cleveland Street
Clearwater, FL 33755
Phone: (727) 447-4454 or
   (800) 583-9523
Web site: www.healthyhome.com

Alternative rug shampoos, paint removers without methylene chloride

Yemm and Hart Green Materials

1417 Madison 308
Marquand, MO 63655-9153
Phone: (573) 783-5434
Fax: (573) 783-7544
Web site: www.yemmhart.com

Organization that gives information about and samples of building materials, furniture, and other products made with recycled content

PAINTS AND FINISHES

Benjamin Moore and Company

51 Chestnut Ridge Road
Montvale, NJ 07645
Phone: (800) 344-0400 or
   (800) 826-2623
Web site: www.benjaminmoore.com

"Pristine" no-VOC paint

Chem-Safe Products

PO Box 33023
San Antonio, TX 78265
Phone: (210) 657-5321

"Enviro-Safe" paint

Dharma Trading Company

PO Box 150916
San Rafael, CA 94915
Phone: (800) 542-5227
Web site: www.dharmatrading.com

Nontoxic dyes

Karen's Natural Products

110 North Washington Street
Harve de Grace, MD 21078
Phone: (800) 527-3674
Web site: www.karensnatural.com

Nontoxic paint removers

FABRIC

Babyworks

11725 N.W. West Road
Portland, OR 97229
Phone: (800) 422-2910
Web site: www.babyworks.com

Cotton and wool diapers, diaper covers, wipes, untreated blankets, natural fiber dolls

Designtex

Phone: (800) 221-1540
Web site: www.dtex.com

Fabric and textile manufacturer that employs environmentally sensitive production methods

Earthlings

c/o Gaiam International
321 Hampton Drive
Venice, CA 90291
Phone: (877) 737-8648

Organic cotton sheets, blankets, mattresses, clothing, diapers, bath towels, stuffed animals, cribs, cotton slings, toys

Eco-wise Environmental Products

110 West Elizabeth Street
Austin, TX 78704
Phone: (512) 326-4474
Web site: www.ecowise.com

Organic/green cotton diapers, pads, and covers; nursing pads; organic cotton clothing, bedding, mattresses, and baby slings; organic baby food

Foxfibre

PO Box 66
Wickenburg, AZ 85358
Phone: (520) 684-7199
Web site: www.foxfibre.com

Naturally colored cotton

Real Goods Trading Company

200 Clara Street
Ukiah, CA 95482
Phone: (800) 762-7325
Web site: www.realgoods.com

Mattress covers, organic cotton mattresses and pillows, untreated cotton towels and curtains, rugs, HEPA air purifiers

WINDOWS AND GLASS

Efficient Windows Collaborative

Alliance to Save Energy
1200 18th Street NW
Suite 900
Washington, DC 20036
Phone: (202) 530-2245 or
  (202) 857-0666
Fax: (202) 331-9588
Web site: www.efficientwindows.org
  or www.ase.org

With support from the U.S. Department of Energy's Windows and Glazings Program and the participation of industry members, EWC provides information on the benefits of energy-efficient windows, descriptions of how they work, and recommendations for their selection and use

National Fenestration Rating Council

1300 Spring Street
Suite 500
Silver Spring, MD 20910
Phone: (301) 589-6372
Web site: www.nfrc.org

A nonprofit, public/private organization created by the window, door, and skylight industry; provides accurate information to measure and compare energy performance of windows, doors, and skylights

WOOD AND WOOD PRODUCTS

CSI

One Woodlawn Green
Suite 250
200 East Woodlawn Road
Charlotte, NC 28217
Phone: (800) 421-8661
Web site: www.treatedwood.com

Preserve Plus, arsenic-free treated wood

Country Road Associates, Ltd.

PO Box 885
63 Front Street
Millbrook, NY 12545
Phone: (914) 677-6041
Fax: (914) 677-6532
Web site: www.countryroad
  associates.com

Sells wood exclusively recycled from old barns, delivers throughout the United States

Smith & Fong Company

601 Grandview Drive
San Francisco, CA 94080
Phone: (650) 872-1184
Fax: (650) 872-1185
Web site: www.plyboo.com

Plyboo bamboo products

INDEX

BIBLIOGRAPHY

Books

Alexander, C. *The Production of Houses*. OUP: Oxford, 1985.

Alexander, C. *A Timeless Way of Building*. OUP: Oxford, 1979.

Anik, D., Boonstra, C., and Mak, J. *Handbook of Sustainable Building*. James & James (Science Publishers): London, 1998.

Ashton, John, and Laura, Ron. *The Perils of Progress*. ZED Books: London, 1999

Berge, B. *Ecology of Building Materials*. Architectural Press: Oxford, 2000.

Borer, P., and Harris, C. *The Whole House Book* CAT: Powys, 1998. (*Probably the most comprehensive and accessible book on ecological building*)

Carson, R. *Silent Spring*. Penguin Books: London, 1999.

Clifton-Taylor, A. *The Pattern of English Building*. Faber & Faber: London, 1987.

Cofaigh, E. O., Olley, J. A., and Lewis, J. O. *The Climatic Dwelling*. James & James (Science Publishers): London, 1998.

Harte, J., et al. *Toxics A–Z—A Guide to Everyday Pollution Hazards*. University of California Press: Los Angeles, 1991.

Hawken, P., Lovins, A. B., and Lovins, L. H. *Natural Capitalism*. Earthscan Publications: London, 1999.

Hill, Marquita K. *Understanding Environmental Pollution*. Cambridge University Press, 1997.

London Hazard Centre. *Sick Building Syndrome*. London, 1993.
———. *Toxic Treatments—Wood Preservation*. London, 1989.
———. *VDU Work: The Hazard to Health*. London, 1990.

McNeill, John. *Something New under the Sun*. Allen Lane. Penguin Press: London, 2000.

Myers, D., and Stolton, S. *Organic Cotton*. Intermediate Technology Publications: London, 1999. (*A telling book highlighting the developing world's dependence on the agro-chemical businesses in the developed world.*)

Papanak, V. *The Green Imperative*. Thames & Hudson: London, 1995.

Pearson, David. *The New Natural House Book*. Conran Octopus: London, 1998.

Peters, V. *Stained Glass*. Crowood Press: Marlborough, 1999.

Phillips, A. *Living with Electricity*. Powerwatch UK: Ely, 1994.

Pilatowicz, G. *Eco Interiors*. J. Wiley & Sons: New York, 1995.

Roaf, S., Fuentes, M., and Thomas, S. *Ecohouse Design Guide*. Architectural Press: London, 2001.

Roaf, S., and Hancock, M. *Energy Efficient Building: A Design Guide*. Blackwell: 1992.

Rousseau, D., and Wadley, J. *Healthy by Design*. 2nd edition, Andrews McMeel Publishing, St. Louis, Missouri, 1999.

Seller, J. *Quiet Homes: A Guide to Good Practice*. B.R.E: Watford, 1998.

Vale, B., and Vale, R. *Green Architecture*. Thames and Hudson: London, 1991.

Vale, B., Vale, R., and Perlin, J. *The New Autonomous House*. Thames and Hudson: London, 2000.

Van der Ryn, S., and Cowan, S. *Ecological Design*. Island Press: Washington, 1996.

Weizsacker, E. von, et al. *Factor Four—Doubling Wealth, Halving Resources*. Earthscan: London 1999.

Wolverton, B. C. *Eco-Friendly House Plants*. Phoenix Illustrated: London, 1997.

Woolley, T., and Kimmins, S. *Green Building Handbook*, Vol 2. F. & F Spon: London, 1997.

Magazines

Building for the Future
Journal of the Association for Environment-Conscious Building
Web site: www.aecb.net/magazine

Environmental Building News
Web site: www.buildinggreen.com/products/allegory.html

Environment and Health News
E-mail: ehn@clara.net
Web site: www.ehn.clara.net

Green Futures
Magazine of Forum for the Future
E-mail: post@greenfutures.org
Web site: www.forumforthefuture.org.uk

ACKNOWLEDGMENTS

Author's acknowledgments

Many people have kindly read drafts and offered constructive criticism and corrections—all shortcomings remain mine alone. In particular I would like to thank Dan Davies of Solar Century, Nick Fordy of Berman Guedes Stretton Architects, William and Gabby Lana of Greenfibres, Dr. Kevin Lane of Oxford University Environmental Change Institute, Neil May of Natural Building Technologies, Sue Roaf, Professor at Oxford Brookes University School of Architecture, Peter Tracey of TDP Environmental Engineers, and Christine Wordsworth. Ian Curtis, also of Oxford's Environmental Change Institute, gave valuable comments as well as much needed encouragement.

Many others provided help and information. I hope they will understand my gratitude even if I don't name them all. In particular, I would like to thank Colin Reedy of Metamorf Design, Bill Tippet of Milliken Carpets, Fritz Stroh-Wilde in Costa Rica, Dr. H. Fischer of Auro Paints, Germany, Simon Garrod, Frank De Mita, and Andy Allen. Hundreds of people readily shared information over the Internet, demonstrating the Web's power to disseminate information and assistance. To all of them, wherever they may be, I extend warm thanks. Thanks to Sue Gladstone, Carey Smith, and Frances Lincoln for their patience. Ruth Prentice handled the design calmly and skillfully under pressure as well as ensured a much needed flow of chocolate biscuits. The designation "editor" doesn't do justice to Jinny Johnson's contribution: No author could dream of a more encouraging, calm, and clear-thinking partner with whom to work. All at Berman Guedes Stretton Architects, particularly Roger Stretton, were unstinting in their support. At home, Alison, Philippa, and Zoe as ever matched my obsession with their tolerance: Lavish with support and encouragement, they made the enterprise possible.

Photographic acknowledgments

a–above, *b*–below, *c*–centre, *l*–left, *r*–right

Alan Berman 8*b*

Arcaid/Richard Bryant 1 & 153*r*, 106-107 (architects Gwathmey Siegel), 152-153 (architects GEA); Julie Phipps 7*b*; Alberto Piovano 47, Belle/ Earl Carter 91 (design Alex Willcock/Don McQualter)

Auro Organic Paint Supplies 134*l*

Axiom/Joe Beynon 54*l*; Chris Bradley 16-17*al*; Dexter Hodges 5 & 120 (architect Carlos Ferrater); Jim Holmes 24*cl*, 33*b*; James Morris 20, 28, 29 (architect James Gorst), 81, 126, 141 (architects Ran Studios), 145, 158*a* (architect Claudio Silvestrin); Paul Quayle 32*l*

Barker Evans 57

Deni Bown 97*bl*, 97*bc*, 97*br*

Jon Broome/Architype 18-19, 89*a*, 96*b*, 174-175

© **Tim Coutts** 156*l*

DesignTex 31*ar* (William McDonough Collection), 149*l* (William McDonough Collection)

Christopher Drake © FLL 82

Edifice/Darley 6*b*; Dunnell 24*l*, 24*r*; Jackson 164*a*; Lewis 77*a*; Norman 7*ar*

© **Richard Glover** 14, 17*b* (architect John Pawson), 32-33*a*, 36-37*a*, 37*b* (architect Arthur Collins), 41 (designer Annie Gregson), 88-89*b* (architect John Pawson), 158*b* (architect Sophie Hicks), 165*a*,165*b* (architect Sophie Hicks),172-173

Polly Farquharson © FLL 64*l* (Kelmscott House)

Francisco Fernandez 54-55

Flow Gallery/Andy Keate 154*c* (designer Alison Crowther)

Freudenberg Building Systems 121*al* (Norament), 121*bl* (Noraplan stone)

Lars Hallen 2-3 & 84-85, 48-49*a*, 50*l*, 62-63, 69, 70-71, 73, 117*a*

The Interior Archive/Tim Beddow 75; Jacques Dirand 150; Ken Hayden 42 (designer J. Reed); Simon McBride 64-65 (artist Douglas Andrews); Eduardo Munoz 137*r* (designer Mary Foxa); Fritz von der Schulenburg 65*r* (designer Jed Johnson), 98-99 (florist Barry Ferguson), 139 (designer Jed Johnson); Simon Upton 118 (designers Colefax & Fowler), 159 (designer Ilaria Miani)

Felicity Irons 117*b*

Ricardo Labougle 110*l*, 110*r*, 112*br*, 115*b*, 127, 128*l*, 128-129, 137*l*, 160, 166*b*

© **Frances Lincoln Limited** 166*a*

Lloyd Loom of Spalding 119*b*

© **Ray Main**/Mainstream 49*r*

Antonio Maniscalco 82-83

Matta/Loreta Bilinskaite-Burke 148

MetaMorf Design 154*r*, 169*b*

James Mortimer © FLL 168-9

Narratives/ Jan Baldwin 44-45, 163, 167

© **Mike Newton** 8*ar* (Vitra), 26*l*, 34-35, 104, 168*l* (Vitra), 169*ar* (Vitra)

Clive Nichols © FLL 111*br* (designer Sue Gernaey)

Paris Ceramics 112*ar*

Michael Paul 138

Red Cover/Winifried Heinze 38-39

© **Susan Roaf** 78*b*

Gary Rogers 6*ar*, 8*al*, 21, 22, 24*cr*, 25*a*, 56, 61, 67, 76, 78*a*, 79, 94-95, 96*a*, 97*ar*, 100-101, 103, 109, 116*a*, 125, 131, 149*r*, 164*b*, 170-171

Paul Ryan/International Interiors 13*a* (designers John Saladino & Sharon Casdin), 13*b* (architect Anna von Schewen), 23 (designer John Saladino), 26-27, 37*ar*, 44*l* (designer Jacqueline Morabito), 46 (designers Kastrup & Sjunnesson), 48*b* (designer Marcel Wolterinck), 77*b* (designer Christian Liaigre), 93 (designer John Saladino), 111*l* (designer Caroline Breet), 115*a* (designer Felix Bonnier), 133 (designers D&V Tsingaris), 155*a* (designers Haskins & Page), 155*b* (designer Christian Liaigre)

Sarie Visi/Ryno/Camera Press 134*r* (architect Johann Slee, production Ronelle Mayer), Sarie Visi/Lynette Monsson/Neville Lockhart/Camera Press 146

Smile Plastics Ltd. 171*r*

Fritz Stroh-Wilde 116*bl*

Studio eg. Inc 156-157

Trannon 154*l*

Simon Upton 6*al*

Veedon Fleece Ltd. 121*r*

VIEW/© Peter Cook 10-11, 25*b*, 52-53 (Jestico & Whiles), 68; © Chris Gascoigne 92 (architects Patel Taylor), 112*l*; © Dennis Gilbert 9 (Design Antenna), 17*ar* (Edward Cullinan Architects), 50-51 (AHMM); 58-59 (Child Graddon Lewis), 143 (architects Chance de Silva); Nick Hufton 43 (Peter Bernamont), 114 (Fraser Brown McKenna)

VK&C Partnership 31*al*

Elizabeth Whiting and Associates/Tim Street Porter 119*a*

Zen Flooring Direct 116*br*

Publisher's acknowledgments

Frances Lincoln Publishers

Editor: Jinny Johnson
Art Editor: Ruth Prentice
Picture Researcher: Sue Gladstone
Senior Commissioning Editor: Carey Smith
Editorial Assistant: Zoe Carroll

Proofreader: Elizabeth Tatham
Illustrations (pp.30-31): David Ashby
Diagrams: Andrew Melton, Hamish McMichael

Rodale Inc.

Executive Editor: Kathleen DeVanna Fish
Managing Editor: Fern Marshall Bradley

Executive Creative Director: Christin Gangi
Art Director: Patricia Field
Copy Manager: Nancy N. Bailey
Project Manager: Karen Costello Soltys
Editor: Tony O'Malley
Copy Editors: Sarah Dunn, Jennifer M. Blackwell, Linda Brunner